D1312610

MFA
HIGHLIGHTS musical **INSTRUMENTS**

DARCY KURONEN

pages 2–3 fig. 1 A Middle-Eastern ensemble with vocalist, psaltery (*kanun*), and frame drum players. *pages 5-6* fig. 2 Omnitonic horn, (see page 85)

MFA PUBLICATIONS *a division of the Museum of Fine Arts,* Boston
465 Huntington Avenue
Boston, Massachusetts 02115
tel. 617 369 3438 fax 617 369 3459
www.mfa-publications.org

Generous support for this publication was provide by Elizabeth and Samuel Thorne.

Manuscript copyedited by Denise Bergman
Typesetting by Fran Presti-Fazio
Design and composition by Lucinda Hitchcock
Printed and bound at CS Graphics PTE LTD, Singapore

Trade distribution:
Distributed Art Publishers/ D.A.P.
155 Sixth Avenue, 2nd floor
New York, New York 10013
Tel. 212 627 1999 Fax 212 627 9484

First edition

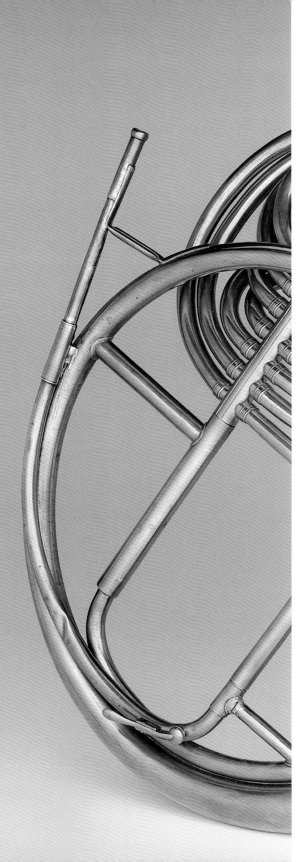

Contents

Director's Foreword

Art is for everyone, and it is in this spirit that the MFA Highlights series was conceived. The series introduces some of the greatest works of art in a manner that is both approachable and stimulating. Each volume focuses on an individual collection, allowing fascinating themes — both visual and textual — to emerge. We aim, over time, to represent every one of the Museum's major collections in the Highlights series, thus forming a library that will be a wonderful resource for the understanding and enjoyment of world art.

It is our goal to make the Museum's artworks accessible by every means possible. We hope that each volume of MFA Highlights will help you to know and understand our encyclopedic collections and to make your own discoveries among their riches.

Malcolm Rogers
Ann and Graham Gund Director
Museum of Fine Arts, Boston

Acknowledgments

It was a tremendous pleasure to work on this book, as I am always eager to spread the word about the Museum's collection of musical instruments, surely one of its least discovered treasures. Moreover, it gave me the opportunity to thoroughly examine a broad range of pieces from the collection and increase my understanding of their design, construction, and history. Information for the entries was drawn from a number of sources, and I take sole responsibility for the interpretation presented here. I am however, most grateful to several colleagues who took time to read various entries for accuracy and who offered valuable new information. For their significant contributions I would particularly like to acknowledge Mitchell Clark, Research Fellow at the Museum of Fine Arts; Christraud Geary, Curator of African and Oceanic Art at the Museum of Fine Arts; John Koster, Conservator and Professor of Museum Science at the National Music Museum; James Makubuya, Associate Professor of Music at Wabash University; J. Kenneth Moore, Frederick P. Rose Curator in Charge for the Department of Musical Instruments at the Metropolitan Museum of Art; D. Samuel Quigley, former Keeper of Musical Instruments at the Museum of Fine Arts and now Director of Digital Information and Technology at Harvard University Art Museums; and Dorie Reents-Budet, Research Associate at the Smithsonian Institution. Several other valued colleagues, too numerous to mention, generously supplied answers to questions that arose during my research.

The book's content, form, and appearance greatly benefited from the dedicated staff in the Museum's departments of publications and photography. I thank Mark Polizzotti for his insightful editing, Terry McAweeney for ably managing the assembly of text and images, and Lucinda Hitchcock for her inspired design. I have always enjoyed working with the talented photographers at the Museum, and I offer my compliments to Christopher Heins, Gregory Heins,

Thomas Lang, David Mathews, Saravuth Neou, and John Woolf for helping to reveal the true beauty of this highly diverse collection from the Museum's holdings.

Finally, my sincere thanks to all those who have supported the Museum's instrument collection over the years, both with donations and with funds that have enabled us to continue building and improving this unique resource. This book could not exist without their generosity and the enthusiasm to see these wonderful artifacts shared with the broadest possible public.

fig. 3 **A Russian peasant playing the balalaika**

Darcy Kuronen
Curator of Musical Instruments

Beauty for Eye and Ear Darcy Kuronen

Musical instruments are among the most meaningful cultural artifacts, reflecting a fascinating marriage of technology, artistry, symbolism, religious beliefs, and, of course, sound production. It is tempting to cast musical instruments into an evolutionary mold, in which seemingly sophisticated examples, like the modern classical violin, would have developed over the centuries from more primitive string instruments. But there is really no natural selection at work here as there is in the animal and plant kingdoms. People create instruments and make choices about what they want them to do and sound like. As human tastes change, so do fashions, including musical ones. Perhaps it is because instruments are essentially tools that we tend to think of the modern grand piano as inherently better than the soft-toned clavichord popular during the Renaissance and Baroque eras. They are certainly very different devices, designed to serve different musical purposes, but therein lies the fascination and delight – the sheer variety of instruments that surround us, from all times, places, and peoples.

fig. 4 Detail from a painting attributed to Nicolas van Haeften, Netherlandish, 1663-1715, *Portrait of a Family in an Interior*, oil on canvas, Charles H. Bayley Picture and Painting Fund, 1982.139

fig. 5 (opposite) Workshop of Evaristo Baschenis, Italian (Bergamese), 1617–1677, *Musical Instruments*, oil on panel, Gift of Arthur Wiesenberger, 49.1789

Given this, we might wonder why musical instruments are often found in art museums, and what their place is there. To be sure, there are many instruments that exhibit beautiful and skillfully applied decoration. Keyboard instruments – with large, flat areas of wooden casework – have lent themselves particularly well to ornamentation, whether a dainty virginal from sixteenth-century Italy (p. 153) or an imposing grand piano made in Georgian England (p. 158). String instruments are likewise often adorned with sophisticated and intricate designs, from graceful eighteenth-century French harps (p. 111) to elegant sitars owned by the upper classes of India (p. 113). At first glance, wind instruments may appear to be less embellished, but often their visual interest is found at a more subtle level. It may, for example, take the form of delicate engraving on the keys of a Baroque oboe (p. 63).

Surface decoration aside, a tremendous wealth of appealing forms is present in the world of musical instruments. It may be as simple as the smooth, polished shape of an African slit drum (p. 36) or as quirky as an English mouth organ made during the Industrial Revolution (p. 73). Even the seemingly plain tube of a bass clarinet has taken on a highly sculptural form at the hands of one inspired Italian craftsman (p. 68). Animal imagery is also widely present. There are ceremonial rattles carved to look like ravens (p. 28), ocarinas in the form of jungle cats (p. 58), zithers shaped like crocodiles (p. 100), and trombones whose sound emits from the head of a dragon (p. 82). The range of materials used in the manufacture and decoration of musical instruments is seemingly endless as well. Virtually every type of wood and metal has been employed, along with ivory, bone, horn, seashells, gourd, clay, glass, textiles, leather, and plastic. Some rather unexpected substances can show up, too, like an armadillo shell used for the back of a small Peruvian guitar (p. 118) or a human thighbone used to create a ritual trumpet from Tibet (p. 78).

Even though musical instruments are primarily created to produce sound, their design, forms, and decoration reveal an exceptionally broad range of artistic expression. They clearly relate to, and may blend imperceptibly among, the many other types of decorative art commonly found in an art museum. As such, their presence in the Museum of Fine Arts, Boston – with its virtually encyclopedic holdings – is at once enriching and exciting.

Musical instruments are appreciated and studied by various constituencies in many different ways. A collector may cherish an instrument because of its rarity or monetary value. To a student of industrial design, it may exhibit a particularly successful and appealing form. Craftspeople will admire the skill required to manufacture an object that requires close tolerances and precise mechanisms. For musicians, instruments are all about sound, as well as the way they respond to human touch. Acoustical engineers may attempt to decipher the complex physical relationships that allow a fine instrument to function the way it does. Among cultures where music plays a more traditional role, an instrument may be admired and revered for symbolic attributes that have little to do with the quality of its tone. Understanding these relationships presents a considerable challenge for the instrument researcher, but it also provides great intellectual stimulation.

Musical instrument makers – referred to as luthiers, from an old French term meaning lute maker – surely experience one of the most intimate relationships with instruments. Through years of training, experimentation, and handed-

fig. 6 William Michael Harnett, American (born in Ireland), 1848–1892, *Old Models*, 1892, oil on canvas, The Hayden Collection – Charles Henry Hayden Fund, 39.761

down tradition, they strive to create an object that is a pleasure to hear, hold, play, and look at. The traditional apprenticeship system has long served instrument makers just as it has other artisans, but there have also been a number of accomplished luthiers who have been self-taught. It is, moreover, not uncommon for musicians themselves to design and manufacture instruments, especially in traditions outside Western art music. Instrument makers understandably tend to congregate in urban areas, but there are many instances in which a modest-size town has become a center of instrument making because of its proximity to a source of quality timber. Regrettably, the costs of labor do not usually allow modern-day instrument makers to lavish as much attention on decoration as their predecessors did. But no matter how well an instrument sounds, both makers and players will still place some value on appearance.

Once they are worn out or outmoded, instruments tend to be discarded, leaving us with relatively few examples from earlier times to help reconstruct their history. Even from as recently as the sixteenth century we have very few instruments that survive in good condition. Likewise, many instruments are quite fragile and don't withstand the rigors of constant use. This is especially true of string instruments, where the body is constructed from very thin pieces of wood. Chronic fluctuations in humidity and temperature over the changing seasons wreak havoc on such wood parts, as they and the joints that hold them together constantly shrink and swell in response to the changing level of moisture that surrounds them. Although instruments have been made of every conceivable material, there is no denying that a large proportion of them are made primarily of wood. The beauty and versatility of wood is attested to in an endless variety of artifacts, but it holds a special place in instrument manufacture, where its distinctive qualities are often critical to an instrument's tone. The relationship of wood and instruments is expressed most poetically in an old motto that speaks of a tree that was mute while alive, but in death was made to sing.

Instruments provide powerful cultural icons, and certain ones have been adopted as national symbols of a country or region: one thinks of the harp in Ireland, the guitar in Spain, and panpipes in the Andean regions of South America. Instruments may migrate across considerable geographical distances during their history, although one must be cautious in drawing firm conclusions about these transfers. For example, instruments indigenous to the Middle East begin to turn up in Europe during the Middle Ages, where they were adopted and developed for local use. Thus we see string instruments like the Arabic ‘ud become the lute, and double-reed woodwinds like the Turkish zūrnā transformed into the shawm, which was in turn a precursor to the oboe.

Free-reed mouth organs brought back to Europe from China and Japan (called a *sheng* and *shō*, respectively) inspired Western inventors to create the harmonica, accordion, concertina, and reed organ. Conversely, a European reed organ called the harmonium has found popularity in the music of modern-day India. Instruments of the Western orchestral tradition have likewise been co-opted for use in much different musical contexts, such as a violin played by a Cajun fiddler or a clarinet used for Jewish Klezmer music. Even the electric guitar has been transplanted worldwide, as performers in Africa play the instrument to express a much different kind of music than do American rockers.

fig. 7 Edouard Manet, French, 1832–1883, *Music Lesson*, 1870, oil on canvas, Anonymous Centennial gift in memory of Charles Deering, 69.1123

The notion of studying musical instruments is relatively new, and as a scholarly discipline it still attracts only a small number of researchers. The majority of music historians and musicologists gravitate toward analysis of music itself, with limited interest in examining the physical means of its production. Many musicians are likewise remarkably uninformed about the structure, mechanics, and history of their own instruments, instead concentrating their efforts on becoming proficient performers. During the past century, however, and especially in the last fifty years, the situation has gradually changed as an increasing number of musicians have taken an interest in how music of earlier times sounds on instruments of the period. And so it has become relatively commonplace to hear Bach or Scarlatti performed on the harpsichord, or music of the Renaissance played on recorders, viols, and other instruments that had once fallen out of favor. Increased global awareness has also led to much greater enthusiasm for what is generally termed "world music." In America's urban centers it is nowadays not at all uncommon to hear concerts of traditional African drumming, street musicians playing Andean folk instruments, and groups performing classical music of Southeast Asia on a gong-chime orchestra called a *gamelan*.

Growth of research about musical instruments went hand in hand with the creation of the world's first major instrument collections during the nineteenth century, among which are those in Vienna, Berlin, Brussels, and Paris. Instruments were likewise incorporated into the holdings of natural history museums during this time, but in these instances they were collected primarily for their ethnological rather than musical significance. As the first catalogues and other publications appeared from the principal European collections, other institutions took an interest in collecting historical and unusual instruments.

The latter years of the nineteenth century and the early decades of the twentieth were an especially active time for the formation of such collections, including the first ones in the United States, which still remain rather few.

The MFA's collection ranks among the oldest in the United States, which includes those at the Smithsonian Institution in Washington, New York's Metropolitan Museum of Art, Yale University in New Haven, the University of Michigan in Ann Arbor, and the Cincinnati Art Museum. In more recent years, a large and significant collection has been developed at the National Music Museum, located on the campus of the University of South Dakota in Vermillion.

The presence of an instrument collection at the MFA came about through rather tragic circumstances. In 1915, a twenty-eight-year-old Bostonian named Leslie Lindsey married Stewart Mason, an English-born merchant who also served as fourth rector of Boston's Emmanuel Church. In spite of warnings in the newspapers, the newlywed couple set sail on their honeymoon aboard the *Lusitania*. As is well known, a German U-boat torpedoed the ship off the southern coast of Ireland, killing over a thousand passengers, among whom were Leslie and her new husband. Leslie's grief-stricken father, William Lindsey, was a prominent local businessman and a trustee of the Museum. We know little of his particular interests in music, but the history and arts of England fascinated him. In one of various ways that he commemorated his daughter's untimely death, Lindsey purchased 560 historical and ethnographic instruments from the noted English collector and musical scholar Francis W. Galpin, and in 1917 donated them to the Museum in memory of his daughter.

Francis Galpin was one of a handful of pioneering collectors and researchers of old musical instruments who began their activities during the mid-to late 1800s. He published various important studies about a wide range of instruments and, upon his death, a group of English friends and colleagues founded the Galpin Society to further interest in musical instruments of all types. That organization continues to flourish today, as does its counterpart in the United States, the American Musical Instrument Society. Galpin's collection contained numerous fine European instruments, but also many Chinese, Japanese, African, Middle Eastern, and Native American examples.

During the nineteenth century, performers began giving concerts on antique instruments, though the practice was mostly considered a novel exercise in recreating history. Francis Galpin was among those who were ardently inter-

ested in the sound of old instruments, and he made it a practice to acquire examples that could either still be played or restored to use. He frequently gave demonstrations and performances using specimens from his collection. A Swiss-born musician named Arnold Dolmetsch, however, is generally credited with most avidly promoting the performance of music on historical instruments. Dolmetsch spent most of his life in England, where he built replicas of harpsichords, lutes, viols, recorders, and other early European instruments. He was a mentor to many musicians of the next generation who took a similar interest in early music and instruments, and most of the members of his immediate family became actively involved in the pursuit as well. Between 1905 and 1911, Dolmetsch lived in Boston and oversaw a special department at the Chickering piano factory that produced harpsichords, clavichords, lutes, and viols. Thus it was that some of the first working replicas of historical instruments hit the shores of the United States, inspiring a selected few to explore music of the past on the instruments for which it was composed.

In cities like Boston, New York, and Philadelphia, concerts of "ancient music" took place sporadically throughout the first half of the twentieth century, but interest in the idea was definitely growing. Of relevance to the MFA's instrument collection, a local performer named Claude Jean Chiasson played a program in 1938 on the Museum's English harpsichord made by Joseph Kirckman in 1798, which included works by Bach, Couperin, and Scarlatti. In 1952, Boston's pioneering harpsichord builders Frank Hubbard and William Dowd restored this same Kirckman harpsichord, which was among the first of many instruments that underwent such treatment in their shops.

In 1941 musical scholar Nicholas Bessaraboff completed an extensive 500-

page catalogue for the MFA, entitled *Ancient European Musical Instruments*, which featured the 314 European instruments from the Galpin/Lindsey collection. The book set a new standard for describing and classifying musical instruments and greatly advanced research in this field. Bessaraboff also advocated use of the word organology (as a division of musicology) to define the specific study of musical instruments, but the term has not been widely adopted. The groundwork was gradually being laid for a school of musicians and craftspeople interested in rediscovering music from ages gone by.

Today, the Museum continues to make its instrument collection available to interested scholars and to craftspeople who want to create replicas. We are, however, also dedicated to preserving the collection in a manner that will ensure its historical integrity for generations to come. To that end, we do not seek to maintain every instrument in playable condition nor always to return derelict ones to that state. Instruments intended for exhibition are cleaned and cosmetically restored to present a whole and aesthetically pleasing appearance, but only a small percentage of the collection is in what can reasonably be termed "playable" condition. Under controlled circumstances, selected instruments are still occasionally featured in the Museum's concert series, as part of lecture/demonstrations, and on audio recordings.

Between 1917 and 1955 only about twenty musical instruments were added to the Museum's original Galpin/Lindsey collection. But over the following decades, Narcissa Williamson, the MFA's first keeper of musical instruments, began to selectively acquire instruments to fill certain gaps. The collection has since essentially doubled in size to nearly 1,100 instruments, encompassing examples from throughout the world and dating from ancient civilizations to the late twentieth century. It is virtually impossible for any instrument collection to be truly encyclopedic in its scope, but the Museum strives for balanced coverage while also seeking to acquire the most significant examples of instruments still available. At present the collection offers an excellent overview of all types of instruments and contains several examples of great rarity, many of which are depicted in the pages that follow.

People have a need to classify things, and musical instruments are no exception. Many classification schemes have been used throughout history (even in the ancient Greek and Arabic worlds) that group instruments together around criteria from acoustic qualities to morphological, cosmic, spiritual, and even sexual attributes. In China, for example, a system was developed whereby instruments are classified according to the material from which they are constructed, using the eight categories of stone, metal, silk, bamboo, wood, earth, gourd, and skin. Within this scheme, trumpets and gongs made of brass are grouped together, as are wooden shawms and clappers. In the 1880s, the Belgian instrument maker and collector Victor-Charles Mahillon created a more scientific system that has become the basis for most subsequent variants. In his system, instruments are classified by the way in which they produce sound, so that wind instruments are grouped together, as are string instruments. In 1914, German scholars Curt Sachs and Eric M. von Hornbostel developed and clarified Mahillon's system, adding a numbering key (akin to the Dewey decimal system for cataloguing books) that allows relatively clear identification of an instrument type without the need to know its indigenous name. This numbering key has been little used by collectors and curators, however. Neither has the cumbersome terminology proposed in much of the Sachs-Hornbostel system, such as "end-blown straight trumpet without mouthpiece" as the proper but lengthy designation for a certain type of Swiss alphorn, or "frame harp with pedal action" for the modern orchestral harp.

The four broadest categories of the Sachs-Hornbostel system have, nonetheless, found currency in musical instrument literature, namely the terms idiophone, membranophone, aerophone, and chordophone. Idiophones are essentially those wherein the body of the instrument itself vibrates and produces sound; this includes objects such as cymbals, rattles, xylophones, and musical glasses. Membranophones make use of a stretched membrane as their sound-producing element, and this category is primarily composed of drums. Aerophones and chordophones are relatively straightforward, respectively signifying instruments whose sound is created by a column of air (i.e., wind instruments) or taut cords (i.e., string instruments). In the twentieth century, a fifth category called electrophones was added to cover the increasing number of instruments that produce sound by means of an electronic signal.

In addition to these main categories of classification, many museums have likewise adopted some of the most general instrument terms used by Sachs and Hornbostel, even though they are often ethnocentric. Thus, in a broad sense, one may speak of lutes from throughout the world as string instruments that have a neck projecting from a body, primarily sounded by plucking the strings. Within this definition, then, we would find the Indian sitar, the Chinese *pipa*, and Afghani *rubāb*, as well as the European lute proper. For the purposes of the present book I cannot avoid my own Eurocentric tendencies, and therefore avoid applying the term "lute" to Western instruments that have ultimately adopted a different name, such as guitar, cittern, or mandolin. This is, to be sure, an imperfect and unscientific approach, and specialists may argue that it does not allow certain instruments to be grouped in their proper category. But the primary aim is to offer basic understanding to a wide range of readers through the use of familiar terms, rather than being completely systematic in naming instruments. For the sake of balance and variety, I have likewise stepped outside traditional classification schemes in the organization of the book's four chapters, grouping the idiophones and membranophones together in a single section called "percussion instruments," and providing a separate chapter called "keyboard instruments." This allows instruments with certain similar qualities to be discussed together and also permits broad representation of the Museum's instrument collection without resorting to placing unusual pieces in a miscellaneous category.

It is difficult to describe musical sound in words, though I have attempted to do so in many of the entries in this book. Fortunately, we live in a time with unprecedented access to recorded music. Those interested in hearing music played on an eighteenth-century harpsichord, a Japanese zither, or a set of musical glasses can access those sounds relatively easily through their local library, record store, or increasingly by way of the Internet. Selecting only one hundred instruments for this volume understandably presented difficult choices. Nonetheless, those chosen offer a reasonable cross section of the Museum's collection, including some of its rarest, most beautiful, and most interesting examples, while still providing representation of the collection's depth and breadth, both historically and geographically. Everyone has a favorite instrument, and I hope that readers will find here both old favorites and new discoveries.

Readers interested in learning more about the MFA's collection of musical instruments can find information and photos for all of the Museum's instruments at its website, **www.mfa.org**.

fig. 10 Israhel van Meckenem, German, about 1445–1503, *Lute Player and Harp Player*, engraving, Harvey D. Parker Collection, 97.1167

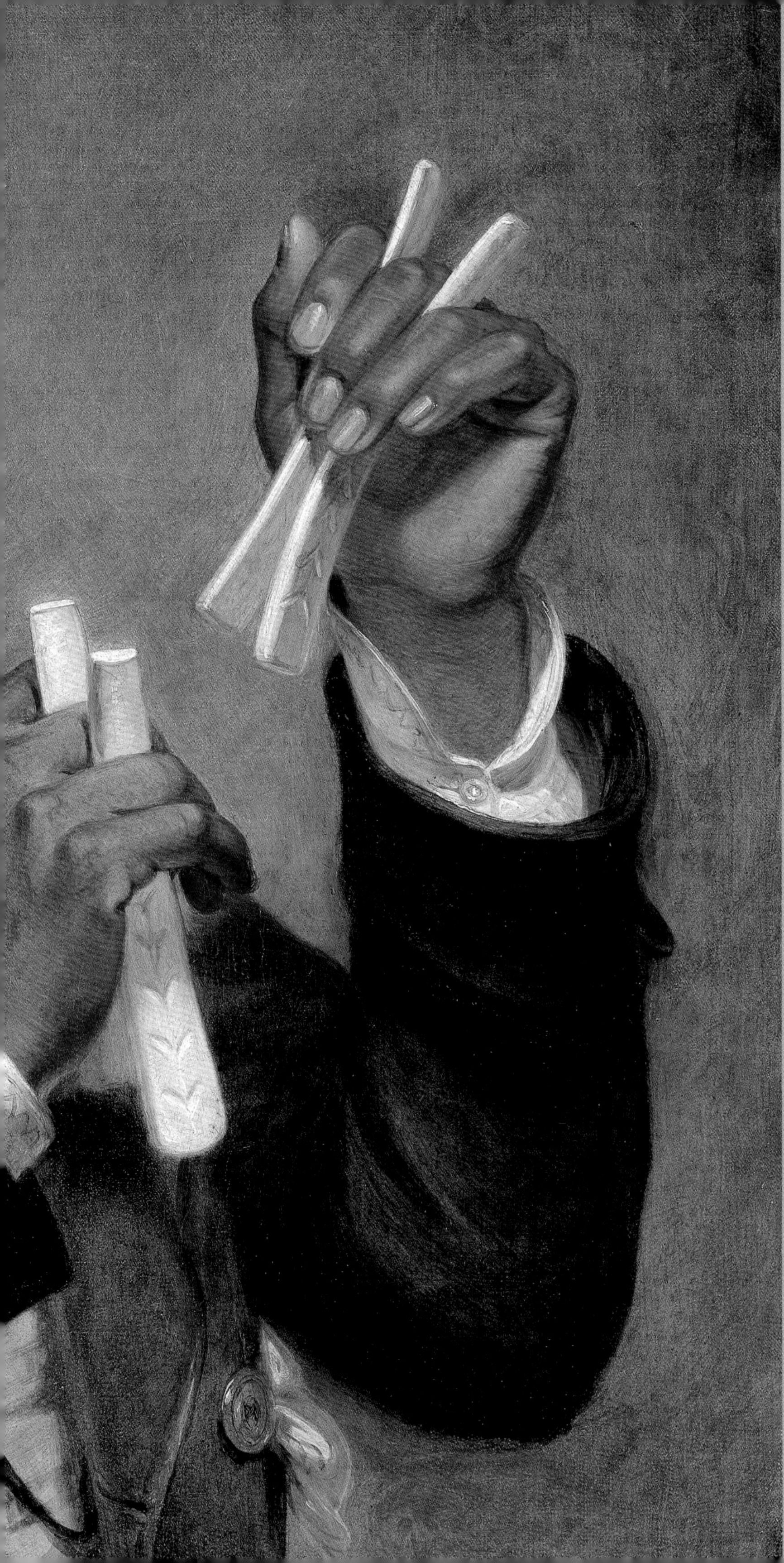

1 PERCUSSION instruments

Percussion Instruments

Rhythm is all around us – in the measured time of each day, season, and passing year and, more individually, in the pace of our footsteps and heartbeats. Was the first musical instrument the human voice, or was it hands clapping and feet stomping in a rhythmic pulse? It was surely not much of a leap for a person to use those same hands to beat out a cadence on a hollow log or, better yet, to use a mallet of some kind. The booming sound produced by tapping on an animal skin stretched on a frame for drying must have seemed especially mysterious.

Although we typically think of percussion instruments as objects that are struck, this chapter includes all sorts of idiophones and membranophones that are also variously shaken, plucked, and rubbed. It is easy to dismiss percussion instruments as simpler than wind or string instruments, and maybe to think that they require less skill to play. Basic sound production may, indeed, be relatively straightforward with these instruments, but true mastery is no less challenging than with any other. Producing the proper sound from a drum or rattle requires a sure hand and an astute ear. And the variety of tones that can be achieved from struck percussion instruments, depending on the player's attack and the relative hardness or softness of the striking implement, is astounding. Not to mention the ability to maintain a steady beat or produce a complex rhythm, especially in consort with others. They say that in comedy, timing is everything, and so it is with percussion instruments.

Percussion instruments constitute a hugely diverse group of objects. The list of indigenous names for various types of rattles around the world, for example, is almost endless. Our catalogue of these instruments becomes even longer, though, when we add countless everyday objects that serve this purpose. Witness the growing number of street-corner musicians who produce remarkable drum sounds from five-gallon plastic buckets. Or stage presentations, such as the theatrical hit *Stomp* where performers revel in the latent percussive potential of everything from push brooms to automotive tire rims to matchboxes.

fig. 11 (preceding page) **Detail from William Sidney Mount, American, 1807–1868, *The Bone Player*, 1856,** oil on canvas, Bequest of Martha C. Karolik for the M. and M. Karolik Collection of American Paintings, 1815–1865, 48.461

fig. 12 (above) **Burmese musicians with drums (*pat*) and xylophone (*pat-talà*)**

To the casual observer, the construction of a drum may seem like a pretty static concept, but here too there is wondrous diversity. Drums may have one head or two. Their body may be shallow or deep, cylindrical or conical, or shaped like a goblet, bowl, or hourglass. They may be played directly with the hands, or beaten with any of a large arsenal of mallets. The pitch of several types of drums can be varied by the player. The orchestral tympani is one well-known instance, but even more versatile examples are found elsewhere. The paired drums of northern Indian music, called *tablā*, produce the most phenomenal range of tone inflection, all with the hands alone. And in Africa, many styles of drum are used to replicate, with some accuracy, the tonal inflections of human speech.

fig. 13 (above) **Japanese geishas playing drums (***shimedaiko*** and *** kotsuzumi***) and lute (***shamisen***)**

fig. 14 (right) **William Morris Hunt, American, 1824–1879, *The Drummer Boy*, about 1862, oil on canvas, Gift of Mrs. Samuel H. Wolcott, 66.1055**

1861. U.S. VOLUNTEERS! 1862.

Rattle

Moche culture

Peru (northern coastal region)

Early Intermediate Period, A.D. 200–600

Along with gold and silver, copper was one of
various attractive metals used by the ancient
peoples of Peru to create jewelry and tools. This
interestingly shaped rattle is typical of belt
adornments worn by warriors and other members of
the Moche culture's ruling elite for ritual performances. It produced a bright, jingling sound
governed by the movements of its wearer. Such items
were important to personal identity and social
standing, and at death would have adorned their
owners in proper attire for the afterlife. Faint
impressions of textile fragments in the surface of
this rattle indicate that it was likely included in a
burial bundle.

Copper alloy
L. 11.6 cm, w. 5.5 cm, h. 2.9 cm (L. 4⁹⁄₁₆ in., w. 2³⁄₁₆ in.,
h. 1⅛ in.)
Helen and Alice Colburn Fund   1984.330

fig. 15 (left) **Detail of Turkish Crescent (see p. 31)**

Vessel rattle in the shape of a raven

Probably Haida people
Canada (Queen Charlotte Islands, British Columbia)
19th century

Like many ritual instruments, this so-called raven rattle is more interesting for its symbolism than for its particular acoustical qualities. There are countless variations in the basic composition of raven rattles, but this example contains all of the visual elements that are considered classic in such instruments. The raven, a mythological hero of Indians living in the northwest coast region of North America, is depicted carrying a box of daylight in his beak, which he has stolen from the chief of heaven. As the story goes, in abbreviated form, the raven then releases the light contained in the box to illuminate the earth, which has previously been in darkness. On the raven's back are a reclining human and a frog; their curious exchange of tongues symbolizes a shamanic transfer of spiritual power. Carved on the raven's belly is a stylized face that some sources indicate is intended to be that of a hawk. Others suggest it represents some kind of sea monster or powerful being. In any event, it is an image of dense symbolism relating to various aspects of social conduct among the people of this region. Raven rattles are also sometimes called chief's rattles, as they are typically used by wealthy headmen to conduct social rituals, much in the way that a master of ceremonies would wield a gavel.

Painted wood
L. 30 cm, w. 8.2 cm, h. 9.1 cm
(L. 11¹³/₁₆ in., w. 3¼ in., h. 3⁹/₁₆ in.)
Gift of Graham Carey   1985.735

Suspension rattle (*shakujō*)

Japan

19th century

The *shakujō* is a type of rattle in which metal rings are suspended from a framework, creating a jangling sound when shaken. Used by Buddhists, it serves a ritual function for accompanying *sutra* chanting and, according to one tradition, the number of rings on the rattle is equivalent to the level that a Buddhist has reached toward enlightenment, six rings indicating one of the highest levels, that of a Bodhisattva. This *shakujō* is handheld, used while seated, though it is also common to find such a rattle terminating the top of a long walking staff. The instrument's metal framework is decorated with various Buddhist images, including groups of lotus petals.

Wood, brass
H. 29.2 cm, w. 6.7 cm, d. 2.7 cm
(H. 11½ in., w. 2⅝ in., d. 1⅛ in.)
Leslie Lindsey Mason Collection 17.2162

Basket rattle

Unknown people
Democratic Republic of Congo
19th century

Rattles are used throughout Africa, though their form and construction generally allow them to be associated with particular areas. Double-headed basket rattles such as this one are distributed throughout central and west-central Africa. Large ones are shaken by the player's hand, but very small basket rattles are sometimes tied to the legs of dancers to provide a rhythmic accent to their movements. A pleasing form, use of natural materials, and skillful weaving all contribute to this instrument's intrinsic appeal as an object, apart from its use as a rhythmic device.

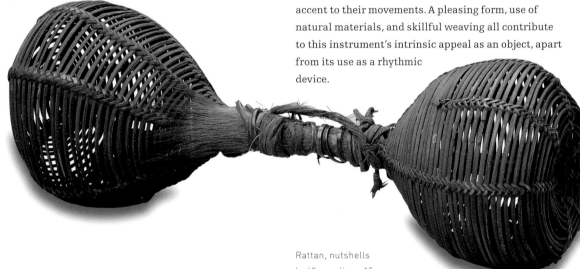

Rattan, nutshells
L. 42 cm, diam. 15 cm
(L. 16 ⁹⁄₁₆ in., diam. 5 ⅞ in.)
Leslie Lindsey Mason Collection
17.2189

Turkish crescent

South Netherlands

About 1810

Turkish bands of the Ottoman Empire were known to use a wide variety of percussion instruments, including kettle drums, bass drums, cymbals, and bells. Through centuries of contact with the Turks, Europeans became fascinated by their flamboyant and exotic-sounding music, along with many other elements of Turkish culture, such as costume, decorative arts, and literature. By the mid-eighteenth century, this taste for "oriental" fashions was growing, as European bands and orchestras adopted many of the Turkish percussion instruments for their own music. The most unusual of these was the Turkish crescent, an ornamented "bell tree" that was used to add brilliance to marching and military music. Also variously called a Jingling Johnny or Chinese pavilion, the bells suspended from the instrument's framework can be sounded by shaking the pole up and down or by twisting it.

   Although made in Europe, this particular instrument retains the traditional Muslim crescent as part of its design. Two horsetail plumes are also often incorporated into the decoration of such instruments. In his ideal instrumentation for a giant festival orchestra of 467 players (outlined in an 1843 treatise), the French composer Hector Berlioz called for as many as four *pavillons chinois* (his term for the instrument) as part of the 53-member percussion section. There was limited call for the Turkish crescent by other orchestral composers, but a similar instrument, the lyre-shaped *Schellenbaum*, is still sometimes used today in continental European wind bands.

Brass, maple
H. 178 cm, w. 39.8 cm, d. 30 cm
(H. 70 ¹/₁₆ in., w. 15 ⁵/₈ in., d. 11¹³/₁₆ in.)
Leslie Lindsey Mason Collection   17.2043

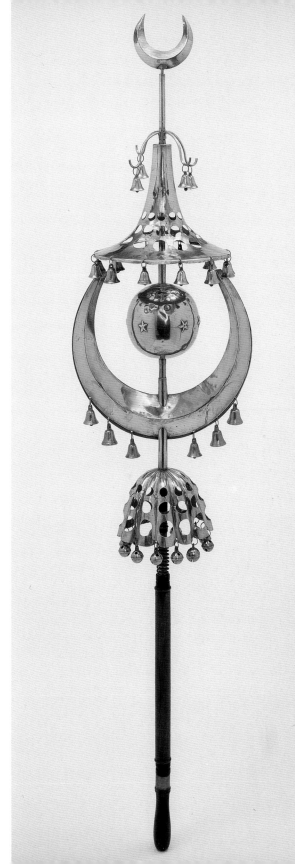

Lamellaphone (*malimba*)

Unknown people

Nigeria

19th century

One of the most distinctive instruments of Africa, lamellaphones are found throughout the continent's sub-Saharan region. Generalists often refer to them as *mbira* or *sanza*, though these are only two of their many indigenous names. Most lamellaphones have tongues (lamellae) made of metal, but cane or wood can also be used, providing a less bright tone. The tongues are arranged so that the lowest tones are at the center of the body, the same arrangement as is found on certain string instruments of Africa. Tuning of individual notes can be adjusted slightly by sliding a tongue farther in or out of its holder to alter the effective sounding length and therefore its pitch. As there are no commonly agreed-upon scales or uniform pitch standard in Africa, the notes are set to whatever pattern is considered the local norm, which may encompass a relatively small culture group.

Lamellaphones are commonly played for personal enjoyment or in small groups to accompany a singer, who is usually one of the players. The tongues are alternately stroked with the thumbs or fingers, hence the instrument's vernacular name of "thumb piano." Even though they are one of the two basic idiophones of Africa that have specifically tuned notes – xylophones are the other type – lamellaphones are nonetheless very much treated as rhythmic instruments. The player may at times use one hand to strike the side of the instrument's body to create a percussive sound. Many types of lamellaphones likewise have pieces of metal or shells attached to their bodies to add a rattling effect. To help amplify the tone, players in some parts of Africa place their instruments inside a large calabash gourd.

Made in a range of sizes, lamellaphones may have as few as five tongues or as many as forty-five, arranged in one, two, or even three rows. The body may be made from a flat board, a hollowed-out block of wood, or constructed from individual pieces of wood to create the top, bottom, and sides (as in the example shown here). The incised geometric designs on this Nigerian *malimba* are characteristic of ornamentation used on artifacts made in the region surrounding the city of Calabar.

Wood, cane

L. 31.6 cm, w. 10.5 cm, h. 4 cm

(L. 12 7/16 in., w. 4 1/8 in., h. 1 9/16 in.)

Leslie Lindsey Mason Collection   17.2188

Jew's harp (*susap*)
Papua New Guinea
About 1930

The twang of a Jew's harp is often associated with rural America, although such instruments are actually found in many parts of the world and date as far back as ancient Roman times. The origin of the name is uncertain, and there is no evidence that the instrument was at any time associated with the Jewish people. Although only one actual pitch is produced when the central prong of a Jew's harp is plucked, by varying the size and shape of the mouth cavity, which serves as a resonator, a player can favor certain overtones to produce the semblance of a melody.

Jew's harps were once played throughout Polynesia for personal amusement, but they have generally passed out of use in recent times, except as a child's plaything. There they are generally constructed from either a narrow stalk of bamboo or a coconut leaf, which naturally divides itself lengthwise to create the necessary form for the instrument. In Papua New Guinea, the instrument is called a *susap*, apparently a pidgin English term. The outer edges of the *susap* are held between the player's teeth, and a cord attached to the base end of the body is jerked rapidly back and forth so that the back of the player's thumb taps the instrument and causes the prong to vibrate. Young men generally play the *susap*, especially in courtship situations, where they subtly "speak" through the instrument as they play it, manipulating the sound to create various vowel combinations that transmit verbal messages. The pokerwork geometric designs on the Jew's harp shown here is typical for decorative arts of Papua New Guinea, and is used on other instruments as well, such as bamboo flutes.

Bamboo
L. 20 cm, diam. 2.1 cm (L. 7⅞ in., diam. ¹³/₁₆ in.)
Helen and Alice Colburn Fund   1984.284

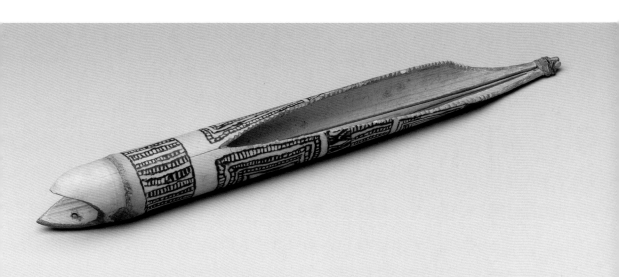

figs. 16 a, b (opposite page)

Indonesian musicians
commemorating the Museum's
acquisition of a gong-chime
orchestra (*gamelan*) from
Central Java

Gong-chime orchestra (*gamelan lengkap*)

Indonesia (Central Java)

1840 and before 1867

These instruments represent a centuries-long tradition of collective music making that still thrives in several areas of Southeast Asia. On the Indonesian island of Java, a *gamelan* ensemble is created and maintained as a group, unified by a consistent decorative concept and distinctive tuning character. Played by a group of about twenty performers, Javanese *gamelan* music has a multilayered texture that ranges from quiet and haunting to loud and stately. The instruments illustrated here are but a few of those used in a complete Central Javanese *gamelan* orchestra, which includes an even wider variety of hanging gongs and horizontally suspended gong-chimes, instruments with tuned metal or wooden bars, drums, and a small group of vocalists. In fact, the entire orchestra (*lengkap*) is actually comprised of two sets of instruments, one made in a five-tone scale called *laras sléndro* (with red casework, as shown here) and the other made in a seven-tone tuning system called *laras pélog*. The Museum's *pélog* instruments (not pictured here) are painted black and exhibit somewhat simpler ornamentation than that on the *sléndro* set. They were apparently constructed sometime before 1867 and united with the earlier *slendro* set, which dates to 1840 and is decorated in a florid, Chinese-inspired style.

Local tradition has it that this *gamelan* was once owned by the Bupati (king's administrator) of Blora, a region located in northeastern Central Java. Whether or not this is true, the quality of the instruments accords with those still found in Javanese palaces, and represents the type of *gamelan* that would have been played in the lavish pavilions of the aristocracy and royal families.

The largest gong in a *gamelan* is frequently given a proper name that reflects its musical or spiritual personality, and the entire ensemble is referred to by that name. The *gamelan* shown here is known as Kyai Jati Mulyå, which translates as "[the] Venerable Truly Noble." Complete *gamelan* orchestras of this age are rare, especially outside Indonesia.

Bronze, teak

Gift of Mr. and Mrs. Bradford M. Endicott and Mr. and Mrs. Richard M. Fraser in honor of Jan and Suzanne Fontein, and the Frank B. Bemis Fund   1990.538–598

Slit drum

Unknown people
Possibly Central African Republic
19th century

Although the use of slit drums is widespread throughout the islands of Oceania, such instruments are equally common in many parts of west and central Africa. They are constructed by cutting a narrow slit longitudinally in a log ranging about two to seven feet in length, then skillfully hollowing out the inside to provide a resonant chamber. Near the center of the slit on this example, two small tongues of unequal thickness are left intact. By striking various areas along the slit with a mallet, up to four different tones can be produced. Although this example is relatively small and devoid of any decoration, it is nonetheless sculpted into a well-proportioned and appealing shape. The sexual symbolism of slit drums is fairly obvious, with the drum's slit representing female genitalia and the mallet that of the male.

Lacking a taut membrane, slit drums are not actually drums in the strict sense of the word. Yet in Africa they are treated in much the same way as true drums and are utilized for similar roles, including imitation of the tonal languages used throughout much of the continent. With certain exceptions, drumming is regarded throughout most of Africa as a specifically male activity. Drummers must undergo rigorous training and carefully observe many traditional customs that surround their esteemed art. They must not only be proficient in their technical and musical skills, but are also required to know a great deal about the history and meaning of their instruments, and the appropriate rhythms for certain contexts. This privileged knowledge of drumming is often passed on from one generation to the next and from master to pupil.

Mahogany
L. 61 cm, w. 21 cm, h. 22 cm (L. 24 in., w. 8¼ in., h. 8¹¹/₁₆ in.)
Leslie Lindsey Mason Collection   17.2013

Hourglass drum

Unknown people

Niger

19th century

At a 1964 celebration of Kenya's independence, a group of twenty-five drummers entertained the thousands in attendance. Noting his excitement at the event, Kenyan president Jomo Kenyata commented that "our life without drummers would be like a human body without a beating heart." And so it is that more than any other type of instrument, drums serve as the heartbeat of Africa, their pulsating rhythms rendering one of the purest expressions of the vast continent's soul and spirit. But the roles they serve are far more complex. There are specific types of drums used for war, work, processions, and healing, while prestige drums are only played at ceremonies relating to chiefs and royalty. So-called sacred drums are used to summon spiritual ancestors, and talking drums are used to transmit information. Many African languages are tone languages, in which the inflection or tone level of a word alters its meaning. By mimicking these tonal variations, a drummer can accurately communicate news and other ideas through the instrument alone. And yet, this information can only be fully understood by those who recognize the particular language being used by the drummer. In selecting wood from which to construct a talking drum, some makers prefer to use trees that grow near a village, since they would most often have been in contact with human voices and would therefore be most suited to "speak" when made into a drum.

Hourglass-shaped instruments of the type pictured here are among the most effective talking drums. They are held under the player's arm (or sometimes against the hip), where the tension, and therefore the pitch, of the thin animal-skin heads can be varied by squeezing the slender, twisted laces that hold them in place. Striking the upper head with a curved wooden mallet, an accomplished musi-cian can vary the sound of the drum with great subtlety. Hourglass drums are also played in percussion ensembles that include other, larger drums, calabash rattles, and sometimes an iron bell.

Wood, animal skin, cloth, vegetable fiber
H. 47.5 cm, diam. 23 cm (H. 18 ¹¹/₁₆ in., diam. 9 ¹/₁₆ in.)
Leslie Lindsey Mason Collection 17.2185

Kettledrums (*naqqāra*)

Saudi Arabia

19th century

Percussion instruments play a vital role in music of the Islamic world, and in many regions rhythmic performance requires a high level of intricacy and finesse. For the tones of a drum, Arabic players distinguish between two basic sonorities of light and dark, with five secondary inflections in between. Rhythmic playing is cyclic, though a continuously repeated pattern will certainly have variation. Through the ages, certain basic metrical patterns have been recorded and codified into a system of rhythmic modes. Some sequences are as short as two beats, while others may have as many as eighty-eight.

There are four basic types of drum found in the Middle East: goblet-shaped with a single skin head, a shallow-frame instrument with attached jingles to color its sound, a double-headed type in barrel or cylindrical form, and hemispherical ones shaped like a kettle. Pairs of kettledrums called *naqqāra* have been played in Islamic countries since the Middle Ages. During the Crusades, such instruments were brought back to Europe, where their name was transformed into "nakers" and they ultimately evolved into the much larger orchestral timpani. Tuned to different pitches, *naqqāra* are widely used in military music, as well as in religious and ceremonial settings. They are sometimes considered a symbol of royalty, especially when paired with trumpets. This pair of *naqqāra* is particularly petite, with footed bottoms that are somewhat unusual compared to most Middle Eastern examples, which are usually rounded like a bowl. To prepare such drums for playing, they must be warmed in some manner so that the sheepskin heads are tightened enough to elicit a crisp tone, as there is no other way to increase the tension of this membrane.

Copper, sheepskin
H. 7.3 and 9 cm, diam. 11.6 and 12.6 cm
(H. 2⅞ and 3⁹⁄₁₆ in., diam. 4⁹⁄₁₆ and 4¹⁵⁄₁₆ in.)
Leslie Lindsey Mason Collection   17.2018a–b

Bass drum

Made or sold by Frederick Lane, 1791–1865

United States (Boston, Massachusetts)

About 1815

The military has long relied on drums to regulate the daily routine of troops, calling them to duty, accompanying their drills, and signaling the end of the day's maneuvers. The various activities are each attended by a specific drum pattern, composed of rhythmic strokes and rolls played on a side drum (snare drum) using two slender sticks, while the bass drummer punctuates the beat on the larger instrument with a heavy, bulbous mallet. Although instructional guides for military drumming were published, the training for most American drummers was by oral tradition up through the Civil War period. An experienced drummer or specially trained drum major would teach his corps of students the necessary rudiments by rote, often in an "on-the-job" situation. It was most often young boys between the ages of 12 and 16 who were entrusted as field drummers in nineteenth-century America, as they were of limited value as combat soldiers.

In the wake of its war for independence, the American government deemed it important to maintain volunteer militias throughout the country. For their periodic drills, these militia units naturally required a set of drums, creating a growing market for such instruments by local manufacturers. The War of 1812 witnessed a particular surge in military contracts, which included an increase in drum making. This well-used bass drum dates from around that time and has an ownership history in the town of Alna, Maine. Records provided by the selectmen of Alna indicate that it is possibly the same instrument that was purchased for the town's militia company in

1820. Many military drums of this period bear some kind of decoration, typically an American eagle, which was often applied by ornamental painters or sign makers. The immense variety of styles and interpretation in these painted designs makes drums like this much admired and highly collectable as folk art.

Ash, calfskin
W. 60 cm, diam. 62 cm
(W. 23 ⅝ in., diam. 24 ⁷/₁₆ in.)
Gift of Charles E. Black and Gale L. Perron, including Karen A. Black, Diane L. (Black) Conners, Emmie Perron-Black, and Katrina Perron-Black   1986.937a–b

Musical glasses (*armonica*)
Probably Germany
Early 19th century

It is not certain when someone first realized that a glass goblet produces a musical sound when its rim is rubbed with a moistened finger. Nor is it known who was the first to assemble a set of such glasses and actually play a tune. But the idea definitely caught fire in the 1740s, when an Irishman named Richard Pockrich gave public performances on a similar instrument in London, which were enthusiastically received. The Bohemian-born composer Christoph Willibald Gluck likewise played "a concerto on twenty-six drinking glasses" at London's Haymarket Theatre in 1746. The ethereal sound fascinated listeners, including the statesman and inventor Benjamin Franklin, who in 1761 conceived the idea of mounting a set of graduated glass bowls concentrically on a horizontal axle and rotating them with a foot pedal and flywheel. This new instrument, which Franklin called the *armonica*, allowed the player's hands to remain stationary as the bowls turned. The *armonica* could therefore be played more like a keyboard instrument, with all of the fingers used to generate multiple notes and chords.

Several musicians took an avid interest in Franklin's improved type of musical glasses, including two female virtuosos, Marianne Davies and Marianne Kirchgässner, who toured Europe performing on their instruments. Mozart composed three fine works for Kirchgässner, and Beethoven specified the *armonica* as the accompanying instrument for a melodrama. Both the *armonica* and the stationary type of musical glasses remained in vogue until the mid-nineteenth century, although there were those who were deeply suspicious that the rapid vibrations of the glasses against the fingertips was causing insanity among performers. The *armonica* may have also gotten a dubious reputation because of the interest shown in it by Anton Mesmer, the originator of "magnetism," who used the instrument as part of his experiments with hypnosis.

Mahogany, lead glass
L. 69.2 cm, w. 33 cm, h. 81 cm
(L. 27¼ in., w. 13 in., h. 31⅞ in.)
Leslie Lindsey Mason Collection   17.2047

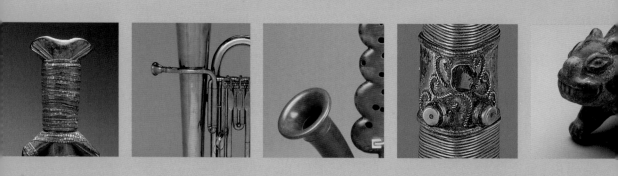

Wind Instruments

Although certain wind instruments are sounded by air pumped with a bellows, the majority are given their musical voice by human breath. As such, these wind instruments allow particularly personal expression from the player and a surprising amount of artistic variation. Although the mechanics of sound production is the same for any given instrument, a player can wield considerable control over the shape of that sound, giving it his or her own distinctive tone. Good tone production is also, however, a high maintenance task, and professional wind players must constantly exercise and maintain the facial muscles that constitute a good embouchure, or mouth position. If everything is in order, one is said to have a good set of "chops."

Wind instruments produce sound through the vibrations in a column of air, which usually takes the form of a tube, but is occasionally vessel-like in shape. Traditionally wind instruments are divided into families called woodwinds and brasswinds, but all wind instruments are actually reed instruments in one form or another. In the oboe and clarinet, reeds made of cane are used as the tone generators. The oboe has two reeds bound together, which, when held between the lips and blown into, rapidly oscillate to interrupt the air stream and set it vibrating within the oboe's body. The clarinet has a single reed that beats against an opening in the instrument's mouthpiece to produce essentially the same effect, though with a much different tone quality. And then there are free reeds, like those found in a harmonica. Here, a small single reed vibrates up and down in a framework without touching anything, but still interrupts the flow of air to make a humming sound. In a brasswind instrument, like the trumpet, the player's lips serve as reeds, again buzzing rapidly to excite the air stream inside whatever length of tube they are joined to. The reed found in instruments of the flute family is a little more difficult to conceptualize, as it is an "air reed." The action of fast-moving air split against a sharp edge gets the air column moving

fig. 17 (preceding page)
Detail from Thomas Wilmer
Dewing, American, 1851–1938,
A Garden, 1883, oil on canvas,
Bequest of George H. Webster, 34.131

fig. 18 (above) François Boucher,
French, 1703–1770, *Shepherd Boy
Playing Bagpipes*, about 1754,
oil on canvas, Given in memory
of Governor Alvan T. Fuller
by the Fuller Foundation, 61.958

in flutes of various kinds. For example, in a modern concert flute (the type held transversely to the body), the air is split against the far side of the oval-shaped blowhole. In a duct flute, like a recorder, the air is channeled through a narrow slit to strike a sharp edge at the opposite end.

Much is said about the acoustic qualities of the various materials that are used in making wind instruments. Performers may contend that gold or platinum flutes sound better than silver ones, or that brasswinds made of certain alloys have a brighter tone. To be sure, materials have an important effect. But at least as important is the way in which those materials are manipulated by the maker: how the bore, finger holes, valves, mouthpiece, and other technical features are shaped.

Woodwind instruments do not generally possess large surfaces that lend themselves to elaborate decoration, but the woods employed are often quite handsome, from golden yellow boxwood to deep dark ebony. Not to say that woodwinds are always made of wood, any more than brasswinds are always made of brass. Metal, bamboo, ivory, bone, earthenware, glass, and plastic have all been used for both woodwinds and brasswinds. In more technologically advanced woodwind instruments, like flutes, oboes, and clarinets, there is also a subtle beauty in the design of their keywork, which became more and more complex during the nineteenth century, as instrument makers developed an extensive variety of key "systems" to facilitate fingering and improve intonation. Orchestral brasswinds, by contrast, are typically a bit more showy than woodwinds, their shiny surfaces of brass, silver, or even gold sometimes incorporating elaborate engraved designs. The long lengths of metal tubing used in many brass instruments also lend themselves to a sculptural approach, and some very attractive forms can be seen in examples of the smallest trumpets to the largest tubas. Just as the elegance of many woodwinds lies in the ingenuity of their keywork, there is beauty in the technological creativity evidenced in the many different valve systems devised for brasses during the nineteenth century.

fig. 19 **Detail from Jean Désiré**

Gustave Courbet, French,

1819–1877, *The Quarry (La Curée),*

1856, **oil on canvas, Henry Lillie**

Pierce Fund, 18.620

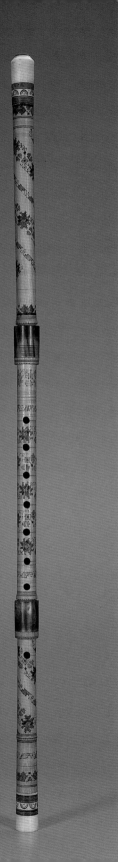

End-blown flute (*kaval*)

Bulgaria

About 1950–70

The *kaval* is a type of end-blown flute in which
the sound is produced by blowing across the upper
end of the tube. Flutes of this type are prevalent
throughout southeastern Europe and much of the
Middle East. Although the tone of the Bulgarian
kaval is soft and velvety, its range is almost three
octaves. Associated primarily with shepherds
and nomads, it is also sometimes used to accompany
dancing. The incised and painted decoration all
along the body of this instrument is reminiscent of
the patterns and colors used in the embroidery
designs of regional textiles and oriental carpets.

Boxwood, bone, horn
L. 85.7 cm, diam. 3 cm
(L. 33¾ in., diam. 1³⁄₁₆ in.)
Helen and Alice Colburn Fund 1984.305

fig. 20 Detail of Tibetan shell trumpet (*dung-dkar*; see p. 79)

End-blown flute (*wua*)

Probably Bwa people
Burkina Faso
Early 20th century

Upright flutes such as this are played together with
drums to accompany dance. They are used in name-
giving ceremonies and other rites marking initia-
tions and funerals, as well as for singing the praises
of chiefs and elders. Each *wua* is limited to a few
pitches and is, therefore, played in sequence with
other, similar flutes to form composite melodies.
These flutes are made in many shapes, some phallic
and others abstractly representing the human form.
Snakeskin wrappings are typical, although there
does not seem to be any particular significance to
the use of this material.

Wood, snakeskin
L. 40.9 cm, w. 8.5 cm, d. 3.5 cm
(L. 16⅛ in., w. 3⁵⁄₁₆ in., d. 1⅜ in.)
Helen and Alice Colburn Fund   1984.296

Panpipes (*antara*)

Nasca culture
Peru (southern coastal region)
A.D. 200–600

Panpipes are composed of several hollow tubes bundled together, each of which forms a different note. As with end-blown flutes formed from a single tube, tones are produced on panpipes by blowing air across the upper ends of each tube. Unlike single-tube flutes, however, the bottom ends of panpipe tubes must usually be closed in order for a note to be sounded properly. Panpipes do exist with a second row of tubes that are open at their lower ends, but this auxiliary row only serves to add resonance to the sound produced from the principal row of pipes.

Panpipes have a long history in Peru, dating back to at least 2000 B.C., and then, as now, they were often constructed from cane tubes. Other ancient examples, especially in the central and southern coastal areas of Peru, were made from earthenware. Although scholars still debate about exactly how the earthenware types were manufactured, it appears that the separate tubes were formed out of clay and then joined together by clay fillings to create a one-piece form. In any event, it seems clear that the makers of these panpipes had enough control over the process to affect the resultant pitch of each pipe to a certain degree, as extant examples produce tonal patterns that are definitely not random. Because of the relative fragility of both cane and ceramic, it is rare to find Pre-Columbian examples that are still intact.

Frequent depictions of the *antara* in ancient artwork suggest that it was a popular instrument, although it was played only by men. Exactly how it was used still remains somewhat conjectural, but it was likely played in ensemble with other panpipes. The *antara* was also apparently very much a ritual object, probably associated with ancestors. Archaeologists have frequently discovered earthenware panpipes in funerary settings, where they seem to have been intentionally broken as a ceremonial act.

Earthenware with red slip paint
L. 45.9 cm, w. 18.2 cm, d. 2.5 cm
(L. 18 1/16 in., w. 7 3/16 in., d. 1 in.)
Helen and Alice Colburn Fund   1984.332

Double duct flute

Colima culture
Mexico (western region)
300 B.C.–A.D. 250

Flutes from Pre-Columbian cultures that lived in the modern-day Mexican states of Veracruz and Colima are often decorated with three-dimensional renderings of humans or animals such as frogs, lizards, and snakes. Although "wet weather" creatures such as reptiles and amphibians are traditionally associated with rainmaking, they may also symbolize rebirth, since snakes shed their skins and frogs are transformed from tadpoles.

Doubled woodwind instruments are found in many parts of the world. In some instances the second tube simply produces a single drone note, while in others it is meant to sound in unison or harmony with the main tube, as with this example. The original owner of this double flute probably trained for many years in a special school in order to provide music suitable for religious rites, events sponsored by the ruling class, and public celebrations. Events like these each required their own musical forms, so different types and sizes of flutes would have been used to produce the tonal range and sound quality appropriate to the occasion.

Earthenware
L. 32.6 cm, w. 3.3 cm, d. 1.7 cm
(L. 12 13/16 in., w. 15/16 in., d. 11/16 in.)
Helen and Alice Colburn Fund   1984.372

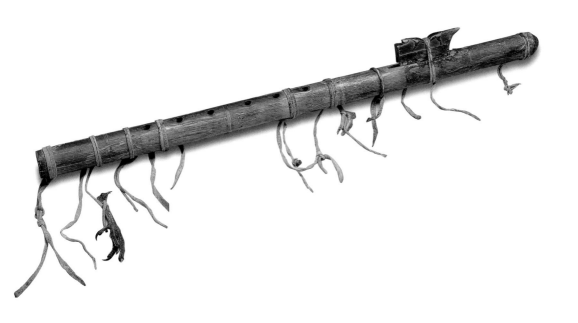

Duct flute (courting flute)
Possibly Sioux people
United States (possibly South Dakota)
Mid-19th century

The "courting flute" used by North American Indians of the Great Plains, Plateau, and Southwest regions is essentially the only indigenous melodic instrument of these culture groups, and is believed to have been in use in some areas for over two thousand years. It was formerly used only by men when courting women, which they did by improvising free and rhapsodic melodies. The flute's body is usually made from straight-grained wood (such as red cedar), spilt in half, hollowed out, and then bound back together with sinew or leather. Examples made from cane are also known, especially in the Southwest. The windway in these flutes is somewhat unusual in that there is a disk or partition positioned part way down the tube, usually carved in place during the process of hollowing the body. This partition is straddled by two rectangular holes, above which is tied a carved block that channels the player's air up and over the partition to set the air column vibrating.

On this flute, the carving atop the block has been variously interpreted as an otter or a horse. The presence of a hawk-claw tassel is somewhat unusual in such instruments, but probably had personal significance for the owner. The 1970s witnessed a considerable revival of interest in courting flutes, and their music has become much better known through the recordings of Native American performers such as Kevin Locke and Carlos Nakai. The instrument's evocative and expressive tone has consequently become a signature sound for almost anything relating to American Indians in film and on television.

Wood, sinew, animal skin
L. 51.7 cm, diam. 2.7 cm
(L. 20⅜ in., diam. 1 1/16 in.)
Helen and Alice Colburn Fund   1984.315

Quintuple whistle (*sk'a'na*)
Unknown people
United States or Canada (northwest coastal region)
19th century

This instrument is from a group of over two dozen whistles and reed pipes from the northwest coastal region that were collected in the late nineteenth century by the English scholar Francis W. Galpin. Such instruments are usually used to imitate the sounds of birds and animals in rituals performed by members of secret societies. Concealed beneath the player's costume or mask, they were not meant to be seen by the uninitiated, and consequently do not bear any decoration. Constructed in an amazing range of shapes and sizes, the whistles can contain anywhere from one to five flues, all sounded by a single mouthpiece.

Red cedar, cedar bark, sinew
L. 39.1 cm, w. 12.2 cm, d. 6.4 cm
(L. 15⅜ in., w. 4¹³⁄₁₆ in., d. 2½ in.)
Leslie Lindsey Mason Collection   17.2208

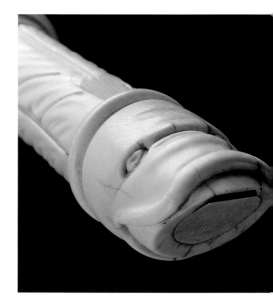

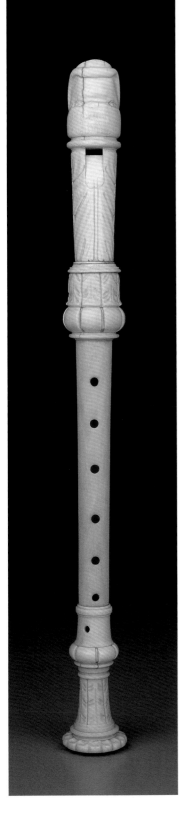

Alto recorder

Germany

About 1710

The recorder is a type of flute with a whistle mouthpiece that produces a gentle and sweet tone, but does not respond well to extremes in loud and soft playing. During the Renaissance, recorders were constructed in many sizes and played in consorts made up entirely of recorders or of a mix of wind and string instruments. By the late 1600s the alto recorder was singled out and developed into a more virtuosic instrument with a considerable solo repertoire; it was also included in many significant orchestral works, including Bach's second and fourth Brandenburg Concertos.

Recorders are still very popular among amateurs and for teaching music to schoolchildren because they are relatively easy to play. This alto recorder is pitched in G, rather than the more common F, and is typical of carved recorders made in Nuremberg, especially by Johann Benedikt Gahn and members of the Oberlender family. The grotesque face carved on the head section *(see detail opposite)* is apparently meant to be some kind of fish staring up at the player. Woodwind instruments made entirely of ivory are somewhat rare, and were probably purchased by wealthy owners primarily for their visual appeal. There is no particular acoustic advantage of ivory over wood, and it is just as susceptible to cracking if improperly handled.

Ivory

L. 43.5 cm, diam. 4.2 cm

(L. 17 ⅛ in., diam. 1 ¹¹/₁₆ in.)

Leslie Lindsey Mason Collection   17.1809

Vessel flute (in feline effigy form)

Guanacaste-Nicoya culture

Costa Rica

Period V, A.D. 500–800

The most common musical instrument found among the ancient cultures of Mexico, Central America, and Andean South America is the vessel flute, sometimes also called a globular flute or ocarina (its European counterpart). Examples with two or more finger holes, which can create multiple pitches, are classified as flutes, whereas those that produce only one note are considered whistles. Likewise, some vessel flutes are constructed with multiple chambers internally, allowing them to sound more than one pitch at the same time. Most of these instruments were made from earthenware and were molded into an endless array of forms, with tone colors and scales equally as varied.

Although often modeled into human or abstract figures, it is equally common to find vessel flutes in the shape of animals, birds, and reptiles. Animals are powerful symbols in this part of the ancient world, and so it was believed that an instrument was endowed with some of that same power when made in the shape of a certain creature. Costa Rican vessel flutes frequently combine animal and human features, suggesting the representation of a shaman transformed into his animal spirit companion. This feline effigy may be a jaguar because the painted rectangular panel on its back contains design motifs similar to the markings on a jaguar pelt. Just as the animal spirit is a powerful force, so is the vessel shape itself, as an object that is able to contain something, whether water or, in the case of a wind instrument, air. Research regarding Pre-Columbian vessel flutes and whistles is still developing, but it appears that one of their primary roles was to provide a call or signal to spirits and ancestors.

Earthenware with red and black on cream slip paint

L. 10.2 cm, w. 5.4 cm, h. 5.9 cm

(L. 4 in., w. 2 1/8 in., h. 2 5/16 in.)

Helen and Alice Colburn Fund   1984.365

Vessel flute (ocarina)

Giuseppe Donati, 1836–1925
Italy (Budrio)
About 1860–70

Flutes in which air is vibrated in a vessel-shaped body, rather than in a tube, are found throughout the world. Because they do not require a tubular shape, vessel flutes can be made in almost any form, and are most often constructed from earthenware. There is no set fingering pattern required on such instruments, as the pitch is determined by the number of finger holes that are covered or open and their relative diameter, rather than the specific sequence in which the player manipulates them. Many vessel flutes have a spout or duct that helps direct the player's breath across a sharp edge, thus causing the air mass to vibrate. In those examples without a duct, the player must direct an air stream across an open hole, much like blowing over the top of a bottle.

The most musically sophisticated vessel flute is the ocarina (Italian for "little goose"), said to have been invented in 1853 by Giuseppe Donati, the maker of this instrument. Donati's first workshop was in Budrio, though he later set up larger manufactories in Bologna and Milan. Budrio itself has remained a center of ocarina production and playing , as various craftspeople there have continued the tradition of making these charming instruments.

Donati's ocarinas have four finger holes and two thumbholes, but cannot be overblown like other woodwind instruments to produce notes in the upper register, limiting their range to about an octave and a half. Donati produced ocarinas in a variety of sizes

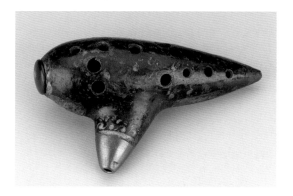

and pitches, however, which when played as a group can render music with full harmony. In fact, soon after developing the ocarina, he and others formed professional ocarina ensembles, some of which became world famous, performing at London's Crystal Palace, the Moulin Rouge in Paris, and for the Czarist court in Russia. Their repertoire included original folk music written for ocarina and arrangements of operatic tunes. The pleasing sound of the ocarina soon caught on worldwide, and could be found everywhere from the schoolyard to the battlefield. Bing Crosby, among others, played the ocarina as a novelty instrument during the Jazz Age, referring to it as the "sweet potato pipe."

Earthenware

L. 14.2 cm, diam. 4.5 cm (L. 5 9/16 in., diam. 1 3/4 in.)

Leslie Lindsey Mason Collection   17.1835

Flute

Marked: *Chevalier*

France

About 1700

It has long been held that a French family of musicians and instrument makers named Hotteterre was responsible for many fundamental improvements in woodwind instruments played during the mid-seventeenth century. Whether or not this is true, the Hotteterres were certainly very influential musicians at the court of Louis XIV, and Jacques Hotteterre published an important method book for the flute in 1707. It is known that the recorder, flute, oboe, and bassoon were all transformed and refined from earlier prototypes into instruments that were more

shown that this particular instrument is one of only a handful of authentic French flutes surviving from this important transitional period, though regrettably nothing whatsoever has been discovered about the identity of the craftsman named Chevalier who stamped his name on it.

Boxwood, ivory, brass

L. 69.4 cm, diam. 3.7 cm

(L. 27 5/16 in., diam. 1 7/16 in.)

Leslie Lindsey Mason Collection   17.1846

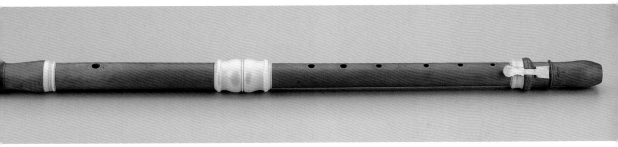

sophisticated in construction and much more versatile musically. The flute, for example, was modified from a simple, one-piece, cylindrical tube into a multipiece, conical-bore instrument like the one shown here, which had bold, elegant turnery.

The flute grew in popularity throughout the eighteenth century, with devotees as prominent as Frederick the Great of Prussia. Along with many other notable musicians, Frederick retained the virtuoso flutist Johann Joachim Quantz at his Potsdam court. Quantz served as Frederick's teacher, composed countless works for the king to perform, and issued his own monumental treatise on the subject of flute playing in 1752. Since the Baroque era the flute has continued to be one of the most popular solo wind instruments, and many of its finest makers have worked in France and Germany. Recent research has

Flute

Claude Laurent, working 1805–1848
France (Paris)
1837

Claude Laurent patented the use of crystal glass for flutes in 1806, recognizing that it was a more stable material than wood in its reaction to changes in humidity from the atmosphere and the player's breath. The tone, however, is not strikingly different from that of a wooden instrument. Over the next forty-two years he produced numerous glass flutes, over one hundred of which are known to survive. Although two of France's best-known flutists of the time, Louis Drouet and Louis Dorus, were among Laurent's clientele, these elegant instruments were mostly owned by wealthy amateurs, some of whom were from the highest levels of European society, including Napoleon Bonaparte, Louis Bonaparte (King of Holland), Joseph Bonaparte (King of Naples and Spain), Louis XVIII (King of France), Franz I (Emperor of Austria), and General Lafayette.

Laurent included the date of manufacture on each of his flutes, which is rare among woodwind makers. Depending on when they were made and the needs of the player, his flutes contain a varying number of keys; generally speaking, more were added as the nineteenth century progressed. Laurent's glass flutes also exhibit an assortment of decorative treatments to the glass itself. Like the one illustrated here, some have delicately cut grooves (called fluting) along their length, while others were made with a faceted diamond pattern. A few rare examples are made with colored glass, and some even have gemstones mounted on their keys. This particular instrument is in a remarkably fine state of preservation, probably indicating that it was rarely played.

Glass, silver
L. 61.6 cm, diam. 3 cm
(L. 24 ¼ in., diam. 1 ³⁄₁₆ in.)
Arthur Tracy Cabot Fund   1994.241

Set of reed pipes (*auloi*)

Sudan (Meroë)

About 10–0 B.C.

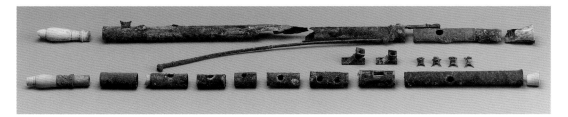

The principal wind instrument of antiquity was a reed pipe comprised of two separate tubes held in a divergent manner, like the one illustrated here on a painted vase of the period. Although the two pipes are held separately in each hand, they are played simultaneously, each with its own reed inserted into the top end. Scholars have yet to agree about whether this was a double reed (like that used in an oboe) or a single "idioglot" reed made from a short piece of hollow cane in which a narrow tongue (the "reed") is cut directly into the surface of the cane tube. The principle of such pipes survives today in certain instruments of the Mediterranean region, such as the *arghūl* and *zummāra*, which are made from tubes of cane. In ancient Greece this type of instrument was called an *aulos*; it is documented from at least the third millennium B.C., and possibly existed much earlier.

The fragments illustrated here are from a cache of *auloi* excavated by the Museum in 1921 from the stairway leading to the burial chamber of a pyramid at Meroë (in present-day Sudan), built for the Nubian queen Amanishakheto. Fragments of *auloi* have been documented in at least five hundred museums throughout the world, but the Museum's set represents by far the largest number – at least sixteen separate pipes in all – ever found together. These instruments were likely the complete equipment of a professional musician who participated in the queen's funeral music. Meroë was on the fringes of the Roman world, but the workmanship of these instruments shows a metropolitan quality and sophistication. In the photograph shown here, a small selection of the many surviving pieces of tubing have been positioned only to suggest the general appearance of the instruments. Much careful conservation and research will be required before it can be known more precisely how all the actual pieces originally fit together.

Bone, wood, bronze

Harvard University-Museum of Fine Arts Expedition

24.1821

fig. 21 Detail from red-figured vase (*pelike*) of *auloi* player, painted by Euphronios, about 520–515 B.C., ceramic, Robert J. Edwards Funds, 1973.88

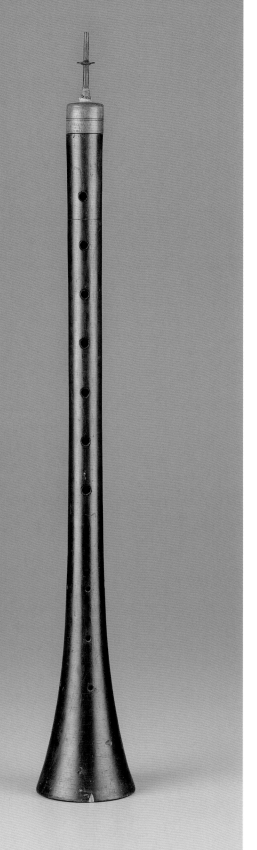

Oboe (*zūrnā*)

Turkey

19th century

Oboelike instruments with a double-reed mouthpiece were present in the Middle East and other parts of Asia at an early date, and by the Middle Ages were transplanted to Europe, where they were called shawms. Other Asian examples of this type of reed instrument are linguistically linked to the *zūrnā* by the similarity of their names, including the *suona* of China, the *sarunai* of West Malaysia, and the *ūahnāī* of India.

The double reed of the *zūrnā* is taken completely in the performer's mouth and is not controlled by the lips, as with the modern orchestral oboe. Consequently, the instrument's range is only about one and a half octaves, and the tone (depending on the player's ability) can be bright, powerful, and sometimes strident. To help support the performer's lips and cheeks from the great air pressure produced, the reed is often surrounded by a disk at its base, against which the player can press his mouth when playing. Called a pirouette, this disk may be made of bone, wood, metal, plastic, or even a large coin. Drilled into the bell of the *zūrnā* are several small holes, referred to as demon's or devil's holes. Although their purpose is to improve the tone, some players also believe that their absence is unlucky and may cause the body of the instrument to split.

Most *zūrnā* players begin their training at a young age. An important part of their instruction is learning to breathe through their nose while maintaining a supply of air in their cheeks, which allows them to play their instrument continuously without stopping. This technique of circular breathing is used not only for wind-instrument playing in various parts of the world, but in other trades as well, such as glassblowing. The *zūrnā* is almost always paired with a bass drum called the *davul*, and is typically played outdoors for weddings, dances, games, and other festivities.

Apricot wood
L. 57.5 cm, diam. 7.8 cm (L. 22 ⅝ in., diam. 3 in.)
Leslie Lindsey Mason Collection 17.1900

Oboe
Hendrik Richters, 1683–1727
The Netherlands (Amsterdam)
about 1720

Oboes are sounded with a double reed made from two thin slats of cane bound to a slender brass tube, inserted in the top of the instrument's wood body. The range is wider and the tone more refined than that of the somewhat raucous Renaissance shawms from which the oboe evolved. With a tone that blends well with other instruments, oboes quickly became the most prominent woodwinds of the orchestra soon after their invention in the mid-seventeenth century.

The unique oboes made by Hendrik and Frederik Richters are arguably the most elegant examples ever constructed, with bodies of ebony incorporating impressive ivory mounts and delicately engraved silver keys. Nearly thirty such oboes are known to survive from the Richters brothers' shop, and almost all are constructed in this highly artistic manner, indicating that these two talented men must have had an elite and well-heeled clientele. The ornamental turnery of their oboes' ivory mounts is the most striking feature. The mixture of intricate basketwork, scalloped shapes, and reeding was executed with a complex type of lathe called a *tour à guilloche*, which allows the device's cutting tool to move in any direction. Although rarely used for musical instruments, ornamental turning on such a machine was, in fact, a popular pastime in many royal households of the time. Another sophisticated detail of the Richters brothers' oboes is the imagery engraved on the silver keys. On the large, centrally placed C-key there is often a rebus (such as on the present instrument), which has been rendered by one scholar as meaning "Grasp time and learn to know the world."

Ebony, ivory, silver
L. 56.8 cm, diam. 6.6 cm (L. 22⅜ in., diam. 2⁹⁄₁₆ in.)
William E. Nickerson Fund 1985.705

Oboe

Guillaume Triébert (born Germany), 1770–1848
France (Paris)
About 1830

The oboe is essentially a French creation. The name they gave to the instrument is *hautbois*, which means "high wood," that is to say, a high-pitched woodwind. In England the term was corrupted into "hoboy," which was eventually transliterated into "oboe." Like all other orchestral woodwinds, the oboe underwent numerous alterations during the nineteenth century in order to improve its tone, intonation, and facility of operation. Additions and changes to the number and type of keys were particularly common, as instrument makers constantly strove to create a model that would be adopted by the best-known musicians. Although this boxwood oboe from about 1830 reflects the trend toward mechanizing the instrument with more and more keys, there is still considerable delicacy and grace in its design.

Like many other successful instrument makers who have worked in France, Guillaume Triébert was born outside that country's borders. It is said that he was trained as a cabinetmaker in the town of Laubach, in the Hesse region of central Germany, and that he walked all the way to Paris, where he began making woodwinds about 1803. He specialized in oboes, and sought valuable input about his instruments' designs from various professional oboists in Paris, including his own son Charles, and Henri Brod, who played in the city's opera orchestra and was himself an innovative maker of oboes. Triébert's son Frédéric (also a professional oboist) joined his father in business and carried on as head of the firm until his own death in 1878. The Triébert name continued to be used long after that date as well, as the company and the marque were subsequently purchased by the firms of Gautrot and then Couesnon. The excellent instruments developed by the Triéberts inaugurated a period of dominance by French-model oboes that has lasted up to the present day.

Boxwood, ivory, brass
L. 56.7 cm, diam. 5.6 cm (L. 22⁵⁄₁₆ in., diam. 2³⁄₁₆ in.)
Harriet Otis Cruft Fund   1998.1

English horn (*cor anglais*)
Wolfgang Kss (born Bohemia), 1779 1834
Austria (Vienna)
About 1830

Since the appearance of the regular oboe in the seventeenth century, various lower-pitched oboes have also been developed. These have included a model that plays at a tonal interval of a minor third lower, the *oboe d'amore*, as well as a baritone oboe pitched a full octave below. The instrument with the most long-lasting success, however, was one that sounds a fifth below its smaller cousin, bearing an assortment of names that included *oboe da caccia, vox humana*, and *taille* (meaning tenor). What developed into the modern orchestral version was dubbed the *cor anglais*, or English horn.

The extra length required for such an instrument often required that it be made in a curved or angled form in order for the player to easily handle it and reach the finger holes. French and Italian makers generally favored the former shape, while German and Austrian makers preferred the latter. The term "horn" was probably applied because early curved examples were considered akin to similarly shaped hunting horns, but there appears to be no logical association with England that would explain the other half of the epithet.

Tenor oboes were readily adopted into oboe bands of the Baroque era, and the use of two English horns, along with pairs of oboes, bassoons, and French horns, became a popular arrangement for wind octets of the Classical period. Two oboes and an English horn likewise became a fairly common grouping for chamber music, and Beethoven composed a fine trio (Op. 87) for this combination of instruments about 1794. During the Romantic era, the rather dark tone color of the English horn was increasingly employed in orchestral works to evoke a soulful or melancholy mood, somewhat typecasting the instrument in many listeners' minds.

Boxwood, ivory, brass
L. 77 cm, diam. 6.7 cm (L. 30 5/16 in., diam. 2 5/8 in.)
Leslie Lindsey Mason Collection 17.1919

Soprano bassoon (*fagottino*)

Johann Christoph Denner, 1655–1707
Germany (Nuremberg)
About 1700

Although an abundance of different wind and string instruments were in use during the Renaissance period, vocal music still reigned supreme, and instruments were primarily relegated to supporting singers. With the introduction of the new Baroque style of music after 1600, the situation rapidly changed, as formidable music began to be composed specifically for instruments in both solo and ensemble settings. For low-pitched instruments, such as the bassoon, a primary responsibility was to supply the bass line as it was harmonized by chordal instruments like the harpsichord, lute, and guitar. This practice is called *basso continuo*, and it is fundamental to the structure of most music composed until the middle of the eighteenth century. The bassoon was, however, also permitted a more virtuosic role at times, for instance in the thirty-eight concertos that Vivaldi composed for the instrument.

Just as instruments rose to greater eminence during this time, so too did their makers. Although the exact identity or workplace of wind instrument makers before 1600 is almost never known, a number of talented wood turners from the Baroque era have literally left their mark on the flutes, recorders, oboes, and bassoons that they made. Johann Christoph Denner is regarded as the greatest German woodwind maker of the period, and he enjoyed international fame during his lifetime. The detail of his turnery and the design of his instruments' internal bores are considered superior to most other woodwinds of the time. In addition to his prolific output of the standard seventeenth-century woodwinds, Denner is credited with inventing the clarinet around 1700.

Only one documented piece of eighteenth-century music is scored for a soprano bassoon (which plays an octave higher than the regular bassoon), yet numerous examples survive of such *fagottini* (diminutive of *fagotto*, the Italian word for bassoon). It has been suggested that these half-size instruments were primarily used for training children who could not easily hold a full-size bassoon. This is the only known example of a soprano bassoon made by Denner.

Boxwood, brass
L. 63.6 cm, w. 4.2 cm., d. 3.8 cm
(L. 25 1/16 in., w. 1 5/8 in., d. 1 1/2 in.)
Leslie Lindsey Mason Collection   17.1922

Clarinet in A and B-flat

Michel Amlingue, working 1782–1830
France (Paris)
About 1794

Invented in Germany about 1700, the clarinet did not find widespread acceptance until much later in the century. Mozart was the first composer to fully recognize the clarinet's capabilities, though it is featured regularly only in his late works. The instrument's single-reed mouthpiece was sometimes placed facing upward by early clarinetists, the opposite of what is now standard. This particular clarinet is also supplied with separate sections that allow the player to create an instrument pitched in either A or B-flat, as certain pieces are easier to play when using one of these setups.

A number of woodwinds of different types survive from the shop of Michel Amlingue, but since all of his other clarinets are made from more typical boxwood, this ebony instrument may have been a particularly special example. This clarinet came to the Museum accompanied by an intriguing note about its history, written in 1832 by its original owner, Captain Bryant P. Tilden. A sea captain and merchant, Tilden carried the instrument with him on voyages totaling over two hundred thousand miles, including trips to Europe, the Middle East, China, Java, and Brazil. He was one of the officers of Boston's Philharmonic Society in the early nineteenth century, and one wonders if he ever had occasion to play his clarinet with that ensemble or the fledgling Handel and Haydn Society.

Ebony, ivory, brass
L. 71.7 cm, diam. 6.7 cm (L. 28 ¼ in., diam. 2 ⅝ in.)
Gift of Mrs. Henry B. Chapin   38.1750

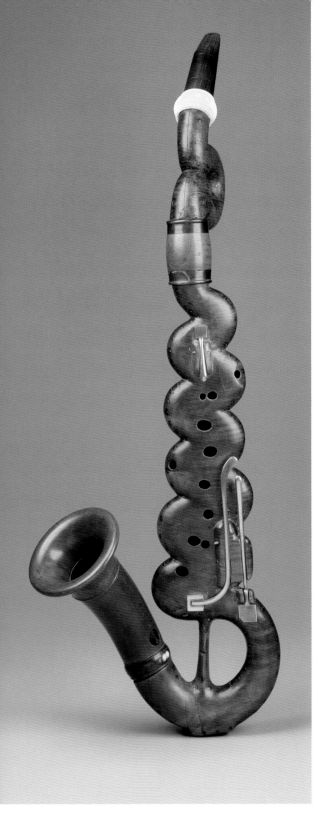

Bass clarinet

Nicola Papalini, working about 1800–1825
Italy (Chiaravalle)
About 1815

Instrument makers have tried various methods of compacting the length required to make a bass clarinet, but this Italian craftsman was alone in selecting a serpentine shape. Nicola Papalini was reportedly trained as a wood carver rather than a musical instrument maker, and he is known only by way of five surviving bass clarinets of this unusual form. The odd pattern of finger holes on the instrument requires the player to cover some holes with the fingertips and others with the intermediate joints of the fingers. The difficulty of construction and scant acceptance of its eccentric appearance probably contributed to this instrument's lack of any real success. It remains, however, one of the most visually whimsical woodwind instruments ever created.

Pearwood, horn, brass
L. 68 cm, w. 21 cm, d. 3.8 cm (L. 26¾ in., w. 8¼ in., d. 1½ in.)
Leslie Lindsey Mason Collection   17.1879

Alto saxophone

Adolphe Sax, (born Belgium) 1814–1894

France (Paris)

1848

The saxophone takes its name from its inventor,
Adolphe Sax, who began designing the instrument shortly before moving from Belgium to France in 1842. Although the
new workshop he opened in Paris was
of only moderate size, he manufactured
a full range of woodwind and brass instruments there, all of
very high quality. Trained by his father, Charles-Joseph Sax,
Adolphe Sax was one of the most inventive instrument makers
of the nineteenth century. He was issued numerous patents
for his work and applied his skills to a wide spectrum of musical and even nonmusical ideas. As an outsider in Paris, though
(and a successful one at that), he faced years of legal harass-
ment from local manufacturers regarding the legitimacy of the
patents he took out for the saxophone and other instruments.
Modern scholars continue to disagree about exactly how, when,
and why the saxophone was developed, but it has been suggested that Sax may have been trying to improve on the ophicleide, an instrument of the brass family outfitted with keys.

This alto instrument must be one of Sax's earliest saxophones, bearing the second lowest serial number (5828) of a
surviving saxophone from his shop. Saxophones are seldom
scored for in orchestral music, but have proven hugely successful in military bands and, more recently, popular
music. It is interesting to speculate what Sax himself would
have thought about his instrument's prominent role in jazz
and rock, musical forms he surely never envisioned.

Brass

L. 58 cm, w. 32.5 cm, d. 14.3 cm

(L. 22 13/16 in., w. 12 13/16 in., d. 5 5/8 in.)

Leslie Lindsey Mason Collection   17.1889

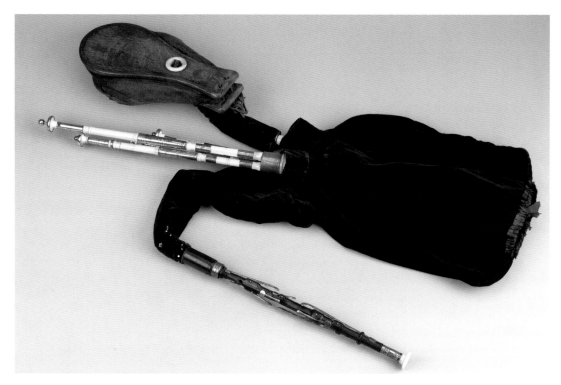

Northumbrian bagpipe
Probably James Reid, 1813–1874
England (North Shields)
1840–60

Although found in many parts of Europe and western Asia, bagpipes are perhaps most strongly associated with the British Isles. The Northumbrian "small-pipe" or "border pipe" originated in the region encompassing northern England and southern Scotland, which includes the English county of Northumberland. This smallish bagpipe is a relatively quiet instrument made to be played indoors, unlike the more common Scottish Highland pipes, whose stentorian sound is so often heard in parades and other outdoor festivities. The playing technique for the Northumbrian pipe is also highly evolved, resulting in music that is exceptionally expressive and virtuosic.

Like most bagpipes, this instrument is composed of a pipe with finger holes for playing the melody (the chanter pipe) and a varying number of other pipes that sound drone notes. The bag of air present in all bagpipes is often inflated by the player's breath, but in the Northumbrian pipe (as with certain other bagpipes) it is filled by a bellows squeezed between the player's right arm and torso. James Reid and his father, Robert, were among the most innovative and esteemed makers of Northumbrian pipes, and are credited with adding several additional keys to the instrument's chanter pipe to allow for a more complete chromatic scale. The most usual pattern, however, is just seven keys (as seen on this example), which allows performance of most existing music for the Northumbrian pipe.

Ivory, cocuswood, silver, oak, leather
L. 84.6 cm (L. 33 5/16 in.)
Leslie Lindsey Mason Collection   17.1933

fig. 22 Albrecht Dürer,
German, 1471–1528,
The Bagpiper, 1514,
engraving, Centennial Gift
of Landon T. Clay, 68.189

Mouth organ (*shō*)

Fujiwara Masaoki, dates unknown

Japan

1715

Inside the bamboo pipes of the *shō* are small brass reeds that elicit a sound similar to that of a harmonica when a performer blows into the mouthpiece. As with many Japanese artifacts, the origins of the *shō* are in China, where its very similar-looking parent instrument is called a *sheng*. Related mouth organs with bamboo pipes are found throughout East and Southeast Asia, all probably descended from the *sheng*, which is believed to date back three thousand years. It was reportedly the French scholar Père Amiot who first sent a Chinese *sheng* back to Paris in 1777, subsequently touching off the invention of several different free-reed instruments, including the European version of a mouth organ, the harmonica.

As the only traditional Japanese instrument that plays actual chords, the *shō* lends a distinctive sonority to the ensemble that performs court music (*gagaku*), playing tone clusters that slowly swell and fade. The seventeen pipes of the *shō* are arranged symmetrically to represent the folded wings of the mythical phoenix, and tradition further holds that the instrument's ethereal sound is an imitation of that exotic bird's cry. Two of the pipes in the *shō* are actually dummies that do not contain any reeds, but are incorporated into the design to provide aesthetic balance. Each functional pipe has a small finger hole near its lower end and a narrow, rectangular vent hole farther up. The thin, delicate reed, cemented over a slot at the base of the pipe, will not sound unless the finger hole is covered, allowing the reed to become acoustically coupled with the pipe's tuned air column.

Marks on non-Western musical instruments that verify their exact date and place of manufacture are rare. A detailed inscription on one of the bamboo pipes in this *shō*, however, indicates that it was constructed in 1715 by a Shinto priest named Fujiwara Masaoki for the Iwashimizu Shrine, which is southwest of Kyoto.

Wood, bamboo, silver

H. 49.5 cm, diam. 7.2 cm (H 19 ½ in., diam. 2 ¹³/₁₆ in.)

Foster Charitable Fund, Samuel Putnam Avery Fund, Frank M. and Mary T. B. Ferrin Fund, John Wheelock Elliot and John Morse Elliot Fund, Alice M. Bartlett Fund, and Joyce Arnold Rusoff Fund   2002.136

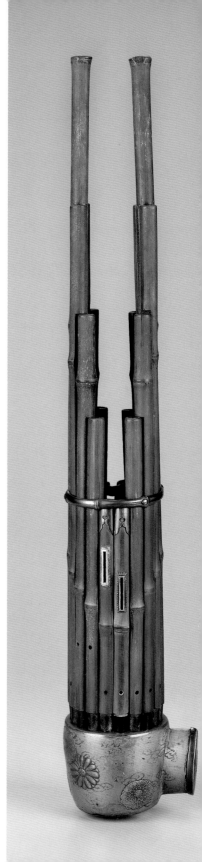

Mouth organ (symphonium)
Charles Wheatstone, 1802–1875
England (London)
About 1830

The English physicist Sir Charles Wheatstone is
famous today for designing and installing the first
commercial telegraph machine in the late 1830s, and
is considered a modern founder of this technology.
But Wheatstone also took an interest in so-called
free-reed instruments like the mouth organ. Although
claims vary as to the true inventor, mouth organs
were being made in Germany in the early 1820s, and
in Vienna by the end of the decade.

Wheatstone's symphonium, patented in 1829, was
one of the earliest mouth organs produced on a commercial scale. Unlike other mouth organs, including
the modern style of harmonica in which the player
selects notes by blocking selected air channels with
his or her tongue, Wheatstone's symphonium has
small ivory buttons that allow air to pass by each
reed as the performer blows into the oval mouth hole.
Petite size and a whimsical shape lend considerable
charm to this instrument, which was available with a
varying number of notes, depending on the model.
During the same period, Wheatstone also invented
and patented the concertina, another free-reed
instrument that likewise has buttons to activate its
notes, but whose air supply is created by pumping a
bellows in and out. Unlike his symphoniums, Wheatstone's concertinas became a big success, and a company bearing his name continued to manufacture
such "squeeze boxes" into the twentieth century.

Nickel silver, ivory
H 5.4 cm, w. 5.5 cm, d. 2.3 cm (H. 2 1/8 in., w. 2 3/16 in., d. 7/8 in.)
Foster Charitable Fund and Helen and Alice Colburn Fund
1996.115

Accordion

Constant Busson, working 1835–after 1892
France (Paris)
About 1840–60

Accordions are related to concertinas, harmonicas, and reed organs in their use of "free reeds" made from brass or steel, which produce a pleasant, humming tone. The accordion's air supply is provided by a set of pleated bellows attached to one side of the body. As the player alternately pulls and pushes the bellows, air is either blown or sucked past the reeds to set them vibrating. In certain accordions, one reed is sounded as the bellows are compressed, but a different one is sounded when the bellows are extended. The keys in early examples are arranged to produce only a diatonic scale, and it was not until 1850 that fully chromatic accordions were produced, using a button-style keyboard. A few years later, a piano-type keyboard was introduced, a feature retained on most modern instruments.

Friedrich Buschmann of Berlin is generally credited with inventing the accordion in 1822, although he called his instrument a *Handäoline*. In 1829, a Viennese maker named Cyril Demian offered an improvement on Buschmann's idea, and dubbed his model the *Akkordion*. Although Demian and his sons were granted a privilege or patent to produce their new design, the instrument's popularity soon led to copies by others, who attempted to avoid infringement by marketing their wares with names such as *Handharmonika*. French instrument makers such as Constant Busson were among the first to manufacture accordions on a large scale.

Although the accordion did not find a place in the nineteenth-century concert hall, it was very popular with musical amateurs, especially young women. Accordions have always been made in a variety of sizes and models, but many of the early ones are relatively small, such as this example by Busson. The modern piano accordion was made and played in great numbers up until the 1950s, but it fell out of favor with the advent of rock and roll and the introduction of the electric guitar. More recently, however, the accordion's second-rate association with polka bands has been put aside, as a new generation of musicians has discovered its unique charm. One can now hear the accordion effectively used in a wide range of styles, from traditional and world music to jazz and pop.

Rosewood, mother-of-pearl, brass
H. 29.7 cm, w. 14.7 cm, d. 11.7 cm (H. 11 ¹¹⁄₁₆ in., w. 5¾ in., d. 4⅝ in.)
Gift of Mr. and Mrs. Joseph G. DeSalvo, Jr., in Memory of
Joseph G. DeSalvo III 1998.100

Trumpet
Probably Roman Imperial Period
About 1st or 2nd century A.D.

This unique trumpet is, perhaps, the Museum's most mysterious musical instrument. It was said to have been found in Greece, near Olympia. But there is no scholarly archaeological record of its discovery, as the instrument was purchased by the MFA in 1937 from a dealer who supplied the accompanying story. Based on the degree to which the bronze has leached into the adjoining bone pieces, the instrument must certainly have been made in ancient times, but precise dating by scientific means would require removal and destruction of a larger piece of the instrument than can be justified.

Made from sections of what is probably cow bone, with bronze ferrules and a cast-bronze bell, this instrument is considerably longer than the military trumpet often depicted in ancient Greek art. The bells of those trumpets are also not shown as being flared like a funnel, but instead terminate in a bulbous shape. Trumpets similar in size and shape to the present instrument are, however, depicted on a Roman relief that is part of the Arch of Titus, located near the Coliseum. Too fragile for field use, trumpets like this were more likely played in ceremonial settings or, perhaps, to announce events at athletic festivals. Indeed, the ancient Olympic games included contests in trumpet blowing beginning in the year 396 B.C. The winner of the competition was given the honor of playing fanfares for the entrance of the athletes, the start of their events, and the crowning of their victories.

In theory, a trumpet of this length could produce a complete harmonic series that would allow a semblance of melodic structure in its high register. As discovered by experiments conducted with a modern replica of this trumpet, however, the very wide throat of the mouthpiece allows the performer to produce only a few different pitches effectively.

Bone, bronze
L. 155 cm, diam. 7.7 cm (L. 61 in., diam. 3 in.)
Frederick Brown Fund   37.301

Trumpet

Tiwanaku culture
Bolivia
About A.D. 500

Although much less prevalent than flutes, straight or curved trumpets are characteristic of many cultures from Mesoamerica and Andean South America. Their forms, lengths, and manner of playing vary greatly from region to region. Most of these trumpets have not survived because they were made from perishable materials such as bark, cane, and gourd, all of which decay rapidly in the relatively wet climates found in much of the area. This wood trumpet probably survived because of the dry, cool, and low-oxygen-content air that prevails in Bolvia's altiplano. It is carved with the image of a standing male figure whose cylindrical headdress recalls those worn by rulers and members of the elite of Tiwanaku, a thriving metropolis in ancient Bolivia, near present-day La Paz. The instrument's very short length and the crudity of construction at the mouthpiece end of the bore suggest that its sound was not of particularly high musical quality, although this may not have mattered to its ritual significance.

Wood
L. 33.1 cm, diam. 3.2 cm
(L. 13 ⅐ in., diam. 1¼ in.)
Mary L. Smith Fund 1986.603

Side-blown trumpet
Zande or Mangbetu people
Democratic Republic of Congo
19th century

In Africa, trumpets that are blown through a hole cut into the side of the instrument's body are far more common than those in which the mouthpiece is at the end of the body. These side-blown trumpets, made from wood or animal horns, are powerful icons associated with worldly power and are used primarily for ritual or ceremonial purposes. Examples made from an ivory elephant tusk are frequently carved with elaborate geometric and anthropomorphic motifs, but they are also quite beautiful when their surface is simply polished smooth. A pattern of incised dots within circles, as seen on this trumpet, is most frequently found in the Vele River region of Central Africa, as is a raised, lozenge-shaped blowhole.

Unlike many African instruments, where the tone is intentionally modified by various means to create a more complex sound, the tone of trumpets is appreciated in unaltered form, though such instruments generally have a limited register of only one or two notes. The instrument's overall length, of course, determines its basic pitch. Trumpets like this may be played alone or in larger ensembles, where they are sounded in a technique called "hocket." Each trumpeter is assigned a particular note or phrase, and sounds it at predetermined points during a performance. This manner of playing is used for other types of African wind instruments as well, allowing a shared creative experience that also helps reinforce certain social patterns and behavior. Tribal chieftains of the African interior retain trumpet orchestras to play court music in honor of their leader. Trumpeters were also called upon to encourage warriors going off to battle, and to greet them on their victorious return.

Ivory
L. 50 cm, w. 8.5 cm
(L. 19 11/16 in., w. 3 5/16 in.)
Leslie Lindsey Mason Collection   17.1960

Trumpet (*rkang-gling*)

Tibet

Late 19th century

The name of this somewhat macabre instrument is a combination of the Tibetan words for leg bone (*rkang*) and flute (*gling*). Although nowadays trumpets of this type are often made entirely of metal (usually with the bell shaped like a dragon head), this example is in the original form, created from a portion of human thighbone, sewn into a skin cover and wrapped with metal wire as decoration. The use of human bone underscores the Buddhist belief in impermanence.

Like most Tibetan wind instruments, *rkang-gling*s are usually played in pairs, primarily in an orchestra of eight to twelve wind and percussion instruments that accompanies Buddhist rituals. The principal melody instruments of the ensemble are double-reed woodwinds called *rgya-gling*s, musically supported by long and deep-sounding trumpets that play pedal tones and two-note calls, marked by ornamented glides and microtonal inflections. Sometimes, however, two of the shorter *rkang-gling*s are added to the group or substituted for the larger trumpets, playing in a similar fashion. The percussion parts are full of rhythmic nuance, creating an overall musical style that is extremely subtle and complex.

Bone, brass, skin
L. 27.7 cm, w. 6.5 cm (L. 10 ⅞ in., w. 2 ⁹⁄₁₆ in.)
Helen and Alice Colburn Fund 1984.283

Shell trumpet (*dung-dkar*)
Probably Tibet
Second half of 19th century

Trumpets made from large seashells are distributed throughout the world, even in locations distant from the ocean, such as the Himalayan Mountains. They may be constructed in one of two ways, either by cutting off the tip of the shell to create a mouthpiece opening or by drilling a blowhole in the side of the shell near its upper end. On the end-blown type, a metal mouthpiece may also be affixed to the opening to provide a more sophisticated interface with the instrument. A wide assortment of seashell species is used in the creation of such trumpets, depending on what is locally available. This particular instrument is made from a shell commonly called an Indian chank, which is found in the Indian Ocean. Shell trumpets are played in many parts of the Indian subcontinent in Hindu temple ceremonies, as well as at weddings and funerals.

The *dung-dkar* is used in Tibetan Buddhist ensembles, where, along with other wind instruments, it is invariably played in pairs. Befitting their role in ritual ceremonies, shell trumpets from Tibet are often decorated with silver mounts and semiprecious stones. This exceptional example is entirely sheathed with silver that is ornately chased with geometric and foliate designs, along with figures of Chinese zodiac animals and the eight Buddhist auspicious symbols. Like most shell trumpets, the *dung-dkar* primarily produces a single strong note, but one with deep and rich resonance that evokes the instrument's ancient past.

Seashell, silver, semiprecious stones
L. 23 cm, diam. 12 cm (L 9 ¹/₁₆ in., diam. 4 ¾ in.)
Gift of Michael D. Wolfe in memory of
his wife, Elise Wolfe 2002.613

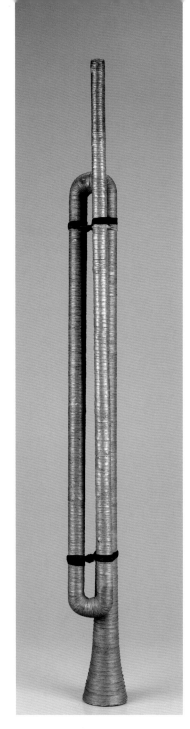

Trumpet (*büchel*)
Switzerland
Early 20th century

It is understandable that the instrument adopted as a national symbol of Switzerland is the alphorn, whose signaling function was once so vital to the herders who roam its high mountain pastures. The most popular and classic version is the very long model with an upturned bell that rests on the ground. But smaller versions were also developed, such as the *büchel*, an instrument in a folded, bugle-shaped form, most associated with the region surrounding Lake Lucerne. The tightly curved shape of the *büchel* is considerably more complicated to create than that of the mostly straight alphorn. Three separate lengths of tubing make up the body, each of which is formed from two pieces of pine stock that are shaped and hollowed out by hand. The two halves are glued together, then wrapped tightly with strips of birch bark to help seal up the bore against air leaks. Since the overall length of the *büchel* is considerably less than that of the alphorn, the pitch is naturally higher.

All types of wooden horns in Switzerland were once used to play signal calls, but in some regions they have also been sounded as a call to church or to battle. Another use for the alphorn was to have one played while cows were being milked, to help calm the animals. Although herders used to make their own instruments, by the early twentieth century individual craftsmen began specializing in their manufacture. Even so, most of these men were primarily farmers and carpenters, who made alphorns as a sideline. Like all simple horns without valves or finger holes, the *büchel* can only sound the natural harmonic scale, where notes occur at rather wide intervals in the lower register, but become closer together as one plays higher up. Certainly the most famous use of an alphorn tune was one heard by Johannes Brahms in 1868, which he jotted on a postcard to Clara Schumann and later incorporated into the fourth movement of his first symphony.

Pine, birch bark
L. 84 cm, w. 7.5 cm, d. 7.2 cm
(L. 33 ¹/₁₆ in., w. 2 ¹⁵/₁₆ in., d. 2 ¹³/₁₆ in.)
Gift of the National Association of Colonial Dames of America in the State of New Hampshire   1989.698

Slide trumpet
England (London)
About 1835

Without any mechanism to alter the overall length of its tubing, a trumpet can be made to sound only certain notes in the natural or harmonic scale. Although notes in the high register lie close enough together to allow performance of a melodic line, playing these high notes requires considerable skill, which is further complicated by the acoustical fact that the eleventh and thirteenth notes in the harmonic series sound wildly out of tune. Over the centuries, brass instrument players and makers have tried various ways of correcting these out-of-tune notes. One obvious solution was to make a portion of the instrument's tubing adjustable by means of a telescoping section. This approach has been used most successfully in the trombone, but was also tried at various times with trumpet-size instruments.

The slide trumpet had its greatest success in England, where it is said to have been invented in 1804 by a performer named John Hyde. By pulling backward on a spring-loaded, U-shaped bend on such a trumpet, a player can slightly alter the length of the instrument, thereby adjusting the intonation of the out-of-tune notes and producing others that are not available on a trumpet of fixed length. Although valves were first applied to brass instruments about 1820 – performing essentially the same result as a slide in a more efficient fashion – there were many noted virtuosos in England who continued to play the slide trumpet until the late nineteenth century.

Apart from an engraved monogram on its bell (likely that of a former owner), this trumpet is unmarked. The slide mechanism appears to have been added to an eighteenth-century trumpet, a common practice. This suggests that the original trumpet was probably a fine-sounding instrument, cherished by those who played it.

Silver-plated brass
L. 68 cm, w. 11.3 cm (L. 26¾ in., w. 4 1/16 in.)
Leslie Lindsey Mason Collection   17.1996

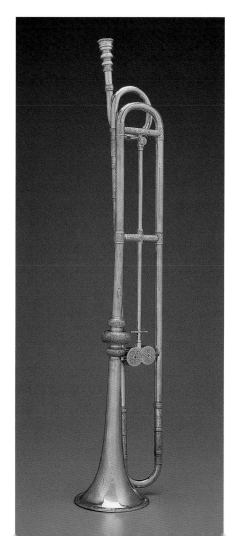

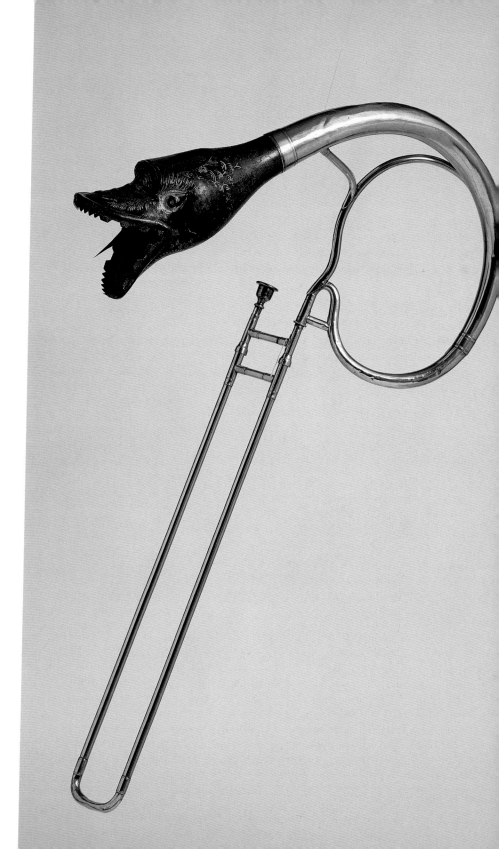

Tenor trombone

Jean Baptiste Tabard, working 1820–1848
France (Lyon)
About 1830

With its telescoping slide, a trombone's tubing can be subtly adjusted in length to produce any required note, which means that as an instrument it has been fully chromatic since first appearing in the mid-fifteenth century. In Renaissance England, the trombone was known by the somewhat humorous name of sackbut. It has been suggested that this word was derived either from the Spanish *sacabuche*, meaning "draw-pipe," or from two old French words that translate as pull and push, and which when combined form the term *sacqueboute*. The appellation "trombone" is Italian in origin, and essentially means "big trumpet." This is no surprise, since the early history of the trumpet and trombone are certainly linked, both sharing the feature of being constructed mostly from cylindrical rather than conical tubing, a characteristic that gives them their particularly bright tone. Since its inception, the trombone has been made in a range of sizes, from soprano to contrabass, but the tenor size is by far the most common.

All sorts of brass instruments with bells terminating in brightly painted dragon's heads were popular with French and Belgian military bands of the mid-nineteenth century. The idea was apparently inspired by depictions of certain ancient Roman brass instruments that likewise had zoomorphic bells, illustrated in a 1780 publication by the French composer and writer Jean Benjamin de La Borde. A trombone of this kind is often referred to as a *buccin*, which is a term borrowed from a type of ancient Roman horn. The dragon's tongue in this imaginative trombone is attached in a way that allows it to wag slightly with the player's movements, a sight that may have startled more than one small child who saw the instrument on parade.

Brass
L. 110 cm, w. 12 cm (L. 43 ⁵⁄₁₆ in., w. 4¾ in.)
Leslie Lindsey Mason Collection   17.2012

Horn

Friedrich Ehe, 1669–1743
Germany (Nuremberg)
About 1710

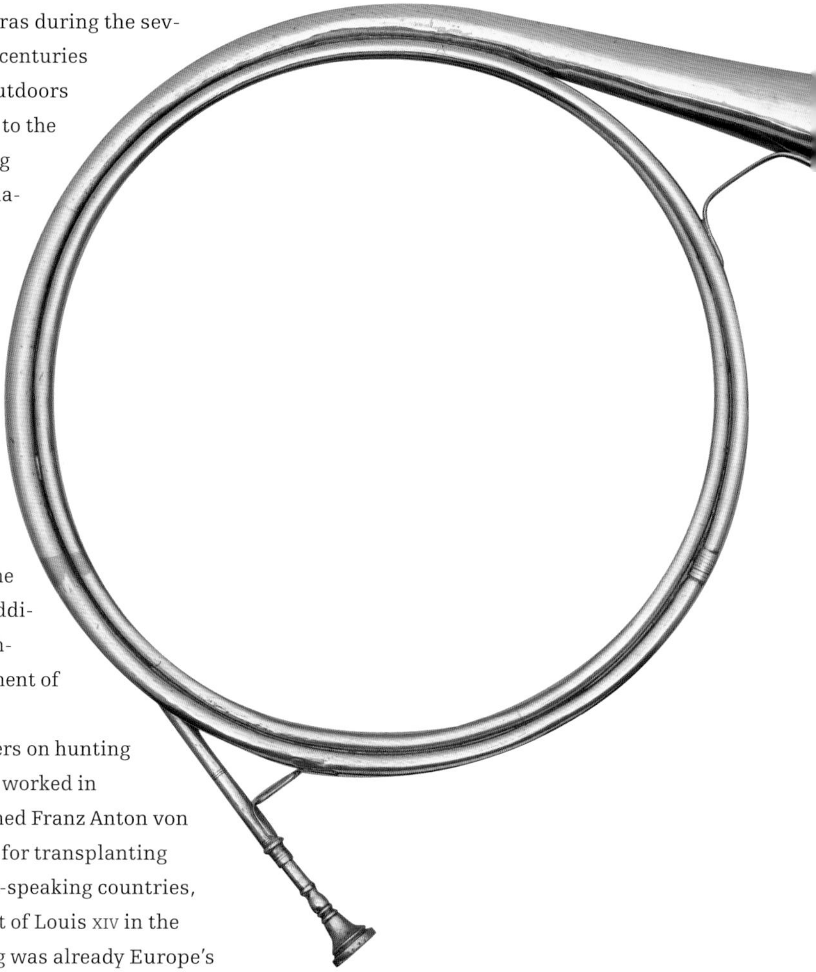

The horns first used in orchestras during the seventeenth and early eighteenth centuries
were the same as those used outdoors
for hunting. They were limited to the
few notes employed for hunting
calls, however, having no mechanism to help produce a full
chromatic range. There are,
nonetheless, some beautiful
and challenging parts for
horn in the High Baroque
works of composers such as
Bach, Handel, and Tele-
mann. By the mid-1700s,
players discovered that placing the right hand inside the
bell opening slightly altered the
horn's pitch, making several additional notes possible. This technique remains a standard element of
modern horn playing.

The most talented performers on hunting
horns during this early period worked in
France. A Bohemian count named Franz Anton von
Sporck is responsible, though, for transplanting
interest in the horn to German-speaking countries,
after a visit to the French court of Louis XIV in the
1680s. By this time, Nuremberg was already Europe's
dominant center for brass instrument making, and
was home to several families who were renowned for
their horns, trumpets, and trombones. This horn
made by Friedrich Ehe is not as highly decorated as
some instruments constructed in the Nuremberg
shops, but it is an especially fine-toned instrument
that players have found "blows" very easily.

Brass
L. 68 cm, w. 22.3 cm
(L. 26¾ in., w. 8¹³⁄₁₆ in.)
Leslie Lindsey Mason Collection 17.1999

Omnitonic horn

Charles-Joseph Sax, 1791–1865

Belgium (Brussels)

1833

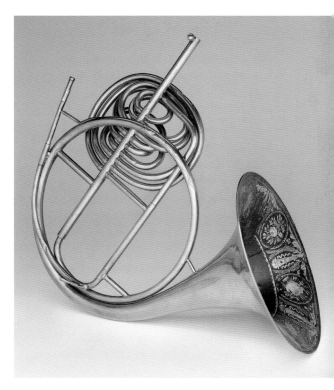

Like other "natural" brasswinds, a horn without valves can only play a limited number of notes from the full chromatic scale, which are dictated by whatever key the instrument is constructed in. In order to have available an instrument that could play in any key, late eighteenth-century horn players adopted a practice of carrying with them coils of tubing of various sizes (called crooks) that could be added to their horns to change the sounding length and thus the fundamental pitch. The system worked well enough musically, but required a heavy wooden carrying case to transport the horn and between nine to fifteen crooks. Horn players of the time were generally conservative, maintaining a deep reverence for the unique tone of a natural horn in which pitch can only be changed by the use of crooks and manipulation of the right hand inside the bell. As a consequence, most performers disdained the adoption of valves, and instead sought other ways to improve their instrument.

A Parisian instrument maker named Dupont was the first to propose a natural horn that is omnitonic (having all tones), in which all of the required crooks are built right into the instrument. His first prototype appeared in 1815, followed by an improved and patented version in 1818. But it was Charles-Joseph Sax in Brussels who developed the most successful omnitonic horn in 1824. In Sax's design, several loops of tubing of different lengths are affixed to the horn's main windway. Each of the loops can be opened or closed by sliding a small knob attached near the upper end of a metal plunger that is pierced by lateral holes at certain intervals. In this way, the player can select the pitch. Although distinctively sculptural in appearance, such horns never became particularly popular, as they were quite heavy to hold and, in any event, were eventually superseded by valved instruments that more conveniently produced a full chromatic range.

Brass

L. 65 cm, w. 29.5 cm (L. 25⁹/₁₆ in., w. 11⅝ in.)

Leslie Lindsey Mason Collection 17.2004

Serpent

C. Baudouin, working 1812–1836
France (Paris)
About 1820

Few musical instruments cause as much curiosity
and bemusement upon first discovery as the serpent.
Although played with a cup-shaped mouthpiece similar to that on other brass instruments, the serpent has
a wood body and finger holes like a woodwind instrument. Its bass tone is mellow, though somewhat unfo-
cused, and was employed for low brass parts in ecclesiastical,
military, and orchestral music until the middle of the nineteenth century. It is
said to have been invented about 1590 by a French canon named Edme
Guillaume, and one can only wonder if this clergyman saw the
irony of creating a serpentine instrument that was so often
played in conjunction with sacred musical chant.

The instrument was not typically associated with virtuoso
display, but in its heyday there were clearly a few players who
must have become quite facile on the serpent, especially if the
etudes published in certain method books from the time are
any indication. In France, especially, study of the serpent was
taken quite seriously, and by 1800 the Paris Conservatory of Music
employed four professors to instruct students in the instrument. But
as other more technically sophisticated brass instruments were developed
during the nineteenth century, the serpent gradually fell out of favor.
The application of certain keys to the instrument, in addition
to its six finger holes, seems to have been only an indication of its losing battle.

Pearwood, leather, brass
L. 85 cm, w. 43 cm, d. 11.4 cm
(L. 33 7/16 in., w. 16 15/16 in., d. 4 1/2 in.)
Leslie Lindsey Mason Collection 17.1954

Keyed bugle
John Köhler II, about 1770–1870
England (London)
About 1835–36

Invented about 1810, the keyed bugle was quite popular in Europe and the United States until the mid-nineteenth century. Like all brasswind instruments, the tone is produced with a cup-shaped mouthpiece, but the pitch is altered by operating keys in the same fashion as woodwinds. The sound is more veiled than modern brass instruments, but accomplished players can perform music of considerable difficulty. The example shown here is pitched in B-flat, but a smaller version in E-flat was also developed, and it was on these higher-pitched instruments that several virtuosi of the day showed off their talents. Among them was America's Edward (Ned) Kendall, who led the Boston Brass Band and was dubbed "king of the E-flat bugle." By the 1830s, cornets and trumpets utilizing valves had become more prevalent, and although these mechanically sophisticated models were ultimately deemed more musically versatile, keyed bugles continued to be made through the 1850s.

This exceptional English instrument by Köhler is made entirely of silver with silver gilt keys and trim. It was presented to Thomas Chamberlayne, Esquire, of Cranbury Park, probably to commemorate his appointment as high sheriff of Hampshire. Surviving with its original mouthpiece, velvet-lined mahogany case (containing a pristine example of Köhler's business card inside), and seven short sections of additional tubing (called tuning bits) to adjust the pitch, the instrument shows very little wear. Chamberlayne probably cherished this bugle more for its appearance and sentimental value than for its sound.

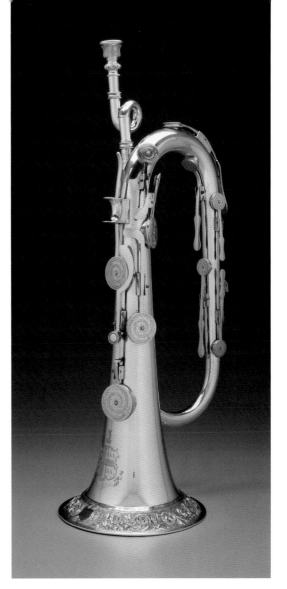

Silver, silver gilt
L. 54.5 cm, w. 24 cm, d. 16.8 cm
(L. 21 7/16 in., w. 9 7/16 in., d. 6 3/8 in.)
Theodora Wilbour Fund in memory of
Charlotte Beebe Wilbour   1986.23

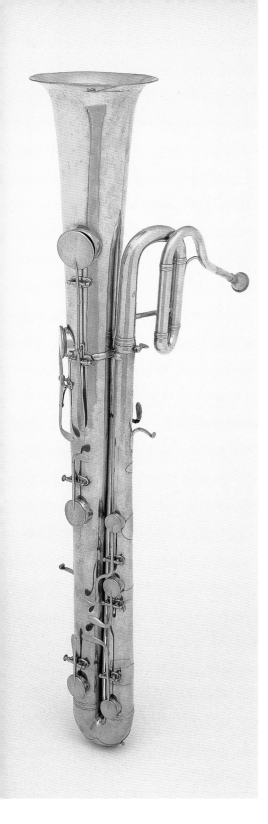

Bass ophicleide
A. G. Guichard, working about 1827–1845
France (Paris)
About 1840

With an appearance that is almost as peculiar as its name, the ophicleide is a low-pitched brass instrument with keys, derived from the smaller keyed bugle and intended as an improvement on the serpent. The name ophicleide is, in fact, a combination of two Greek words that essentially translate as "keyed serpent." But the instrument retains none of the serpent's snakelike curves, instead assuming a folded shape similar to a bassoon. Because its tone holes and the key pads that cover them can be placed at acoustically rational positions along its bore, the tone of the ophicleide is more focused and provides much better intonation than the serpent, where finger holes must simply be placed within reach of the human hand. A skilled ophicleide player can produce a three-octave range, but the instrument requires a great deal of breath, since its very wide, conical bore offers little resistance.

Jean Hilaire Asté (also known as Antoine Halary) patented the ophicleide in 1821, initially proposing an instrument with nine keys, although eleven later became the norm. In a written report, the Academie Française described the instrument's tone as midway between the human voice and the bassoon. Several sizes of ophicleide were produced, including a soprano (extremely rare), an alto (curiously called the *quinticlave*), and a few contrabass or "monster" instruments that stood nearly five feet tall. By far the most popular and useful size, however, was the bass ophicleide, which was still offered in at least one instrument dealer's catalogue as late as 1916. French firms were the most prolific producers of ophicleides, although there were several fine makers in England as well. Throughout much of the nineteenth century the ophicleide was utilized in band and orchestral music, and is included, for example, in the original scores for Mendelssohn's *Overture to a Midsummer Night's Dream* and Berlioz's *Symphonie fantastique*.

Brass
L. 114 cm, w. 21 cm (L. 44⅞ in., w. 8¼ in.)
Leslie Lindsey Mason Collection   17.1959

Cornet (circular model)

Germany

About 1850

People are often confused about the difference between the trumpet and the cornet, which is understandable, since their size, shape, pitch, and playing technique have often had much in common. Even today, there are certain brasswind instruments of this type that elude exact categorization. We may, however, generally define the trumpet as having tubing that is cylindrical for most of its length, whereas the bore of the cornet is conical, gradually expanding all the way from the point where the mouthpiece is inserted up to the bell. The difference in timbre between the two instruments is noticeable. While the trumpet's sound is bright and focused, that of the cornet is rather warm and mellow. The same, somewhat muffled tone is even more pronounced in the larger French horn, which likewise has a conical bore.

There is no patent for the cornet, but it apparently came about when a French maker conceived the idea of fitting valves to the coiled post horn during the mid- to late 1820s. Underscoring the relationship of the instruments is that the root word *cor* in cornet is French for horn. The new instrument was versatile from a musical standpoint, but had trouble escaping

its plebian past. Rather than finding a ready spot in the symphony orchestra, the cornet's gay sound associated it more with military bands, as well as ensembles that played light concert and dance music. Many of the cornet's early virtuosos were former French horn players, as trumpeters initially steered clear of the instrument.

The circular form of the instrument shown here reflects the cornet's ancestral relationship to the post horn. This unusual German cornet was built for a left-handed player and has three so-called Viennese valves, a type patented in 1830 by Leopold Uhlmann of Vienna that employs a pair of slender pistons for each valve. Uhlman's double-piston mechanism was one of several valve designs proposed for brass instruments during the nineteenth century. The Industrial Revolution encouraged such inventiveness and provided the means to manufacture devices like valves with greater precision.

Brass, nickel silver
L. 32 cm, w. 12.2 cm (L. 12 5/8 in., w. 4 13/16 in.)
Leslie Lindsey Mason Collection   17.1988

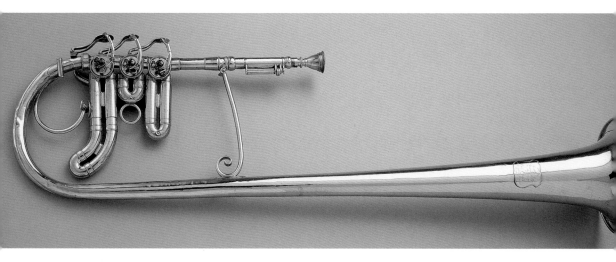

Cornet (over-shoulder model)
Graves and Company
United States (Boston, Massachusetts)
1856

Samuel Graves (1794–1878) was the first American to produce wind instruments of all types on a large scale, beginning in the 1830s in his original factory in Winchester, New Hampshire. After relocating to Boston in 1851, though, the Graves firm concentrated solely on brass instruments. During the Civil War period, many American bands were outfitted with brass instruments that were called "over-shoulder" models, with bells pointing backward to project their sound to the troops marching behind the band. Such instruments were constructed in all sizes, from a high E-flat cornet down to the largest tubas.

This cornet is one of a matched set of twenty brass instruments – constituting the instrumentation for an entire brass band – that was commissioned in 1856 by Colonel Samuel Colt at a total cost of $1,613 for his Armory Band in Hartford, Connecticut. It was common at the time for regimental commanders to organize and outfit a band at their personal expense. Colt was a highly successful manufacturer of firearms, and the emblem on this cornet includes a small engraved picture of a revolver, the type of pistol for

which Colt is still famous today. A period description of the band's uniforms indicates that they are "the dress of the Prussian Rifleman with the Light Cavalry Helmet"; the outfit was completed by a revolver supplied to each band member "for self defense." The *Hartford Daily Courant* zealously called Colt's purchase of the twenty instruments "an act worthy of the Medicis of Florence, in their proudest day."

An unusual feature of this E-flat cornet, and apparently one also included on certain other instruments from the set, is that the valve assembly can easily be detached from the bell. It appears that this allowed the valves to be alternately attached to another bell (supplied by Graves when the instruments were sent to Hartford) that was shaped to point forward in the normal manner, rather than in the over-shoulder configuration.

Nickel silver
L. 55.7 cm, w. 21 cm, d. 11.8 cm
(L. 21 ¹⁵⁄₁₆ in., w. 8¼ in., d. 4 ⁵⁄₈ in.)
Foster Charitable Fund   1991.228

Tuba

Gilmore, Graves and
Company
United States
(Boston, Massachusetts)
1864–65

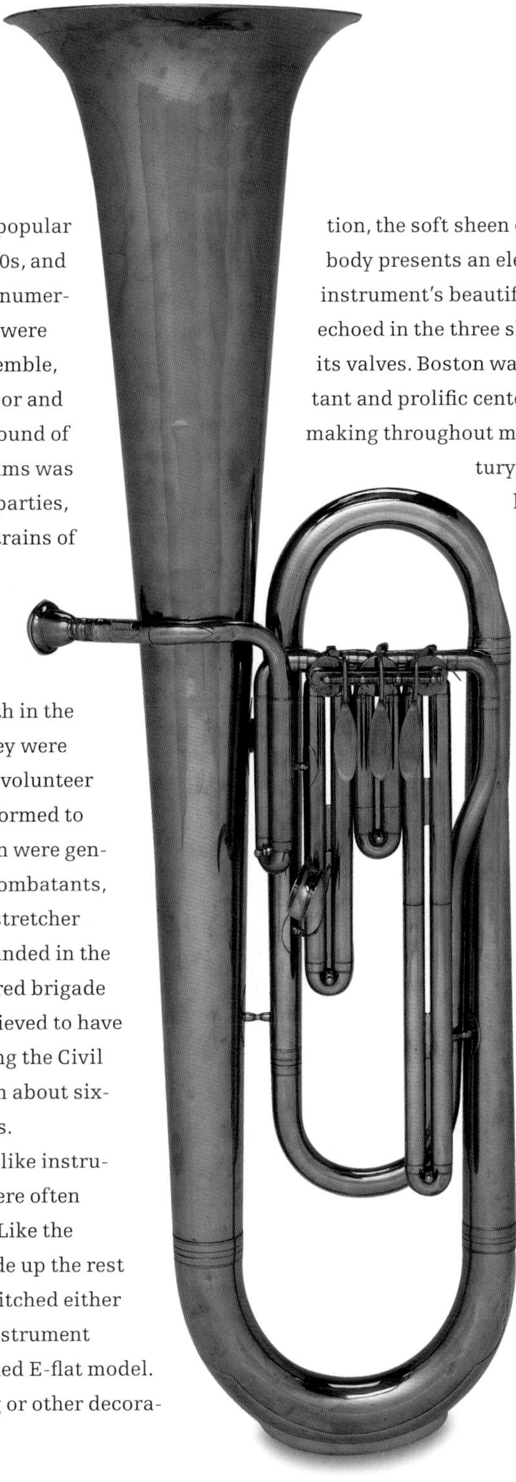

All-brass bands first became popular in the United States in the 1840s, and over the next several decades numerous towns across the country were home to at least one such ensemble, which performed at both indoor and outdoor events. The stirring sound of cornets, horns, tubas, and drums was not only a fixture at parades, parties, and dances, but the martial strains of their music was also a great attention-getter when recruiting troops for a local militia unit. The Civil War prompted considerable growth in the number of brass bands, as they were mustered in to serve with the volunteer regiments that were quickly formed to fight in the conflict. Bandsmen were generally not required to act as combatants, but they often functioned as stretcher bearers and attended the wounded in the wake of a battle. Over a hundred brigade and regimental bands are believed to have served the Federal army during the Civil War, each ranging in size from about sixteen to twenty-four musicians.

The first low-pitched, tubalike instruments used in brass bands were often referred to simply as basses. Like the smaller instruments that made up the rest of a brass band, tubas were pitched either in B-flat or E-flat. The large instrument shown here is the lower-pitched E-flat model. Although devoid of engraving or other decoration, the soft sheen of its nickel silver body presents an elegant surface, while the instrument's beautifully elongated form is echoed in the three slender levers that operate its valves. Boston was one of the most important and prolific centers for brass instrument making throughout much of the nineteenth century, many examples of which have survived in good condition. One of the partners in the firm that manufactured this tuba was bandmaster Patrick S. Gilmore, composer of the well-known Civil War tune "When Johnny Comes Marching Home." In 1869 Gilmore organized a National Peace Jubilee in Boston, a five-day event featuring a thousand-piece orchestra, a chorus of 10,000, and six different bands.

Nickel silver
L. 118 cm, w. 40.5 cm,
d. 28.4 cm
(L. 46 7/16 in., w. 15 15/16 in.,
d. 11 13/16 in.)
Foster Charitable Fund
1996.112

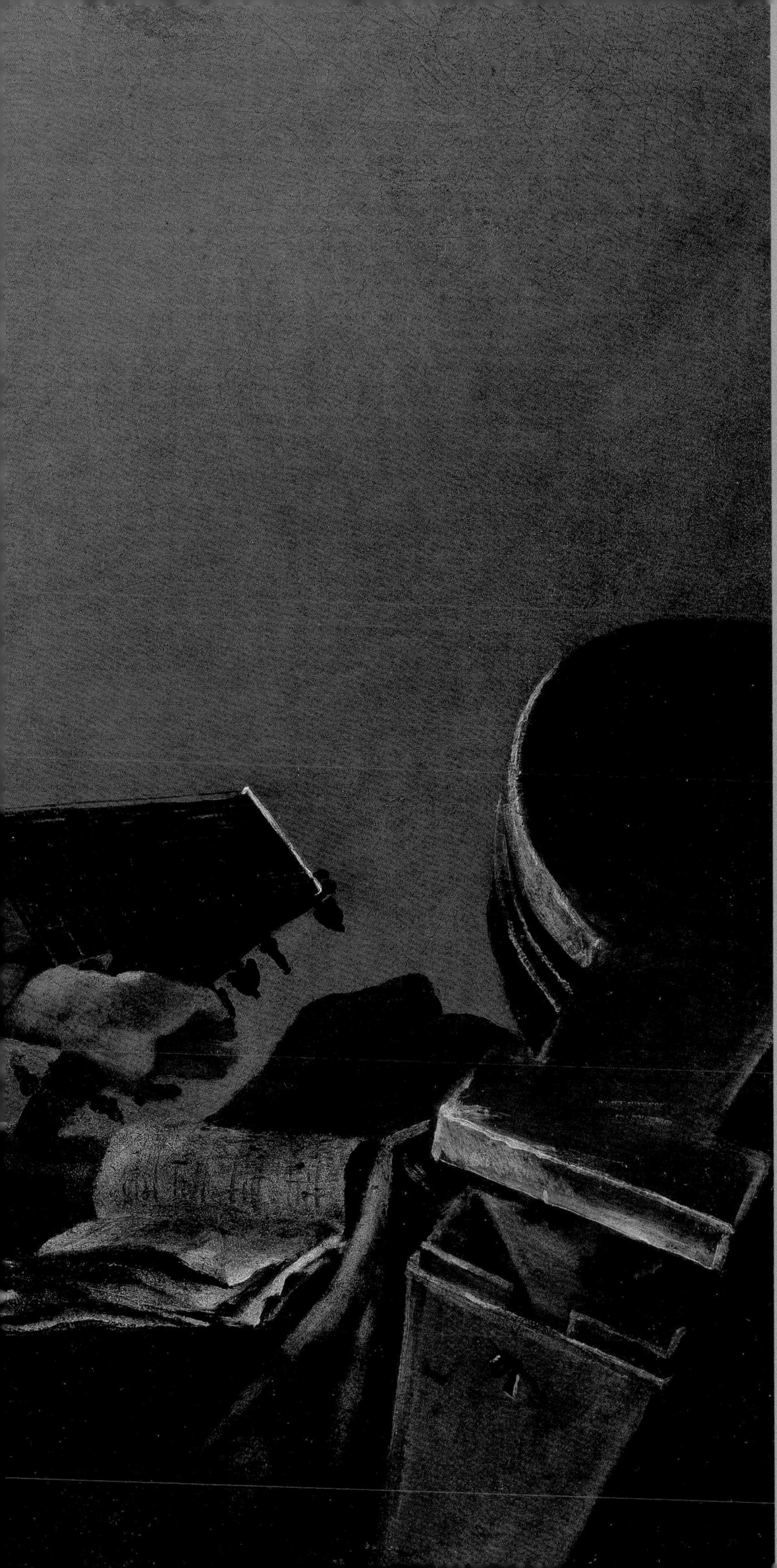

3 STRING instruments

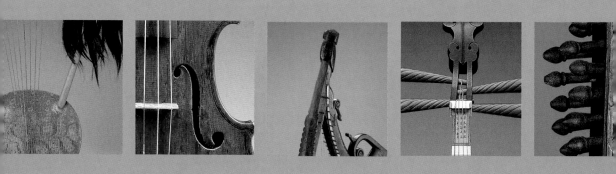

String Instruments

In ancient Greek mythology there is a story of a contest between the god Apollo and a satyr named Marsyas, whose musical abilities were judged by King Midas and the nine Muses. Apollo's lyre was ultimately deemed superior to Marsyas's double pipes, some say because a lyre allowed the performer to sing with the instrument while it was being played. Regardless of how the same contest might be judged today, there is something undeniably soothing about the sound of many string instruments. Is it any wonder we hear so many harps at weddings and at upscale restaurants, or that the lute and guitar have long been the instrument of choice for serenading? String instruments also have a natural appeal to those who play music on a casual basis. Bowing a violin may take a good bit of time to master, but strumming the strings on a zither or guitar (assuming they're in tune) can offer quite gratifying results even for a beginner.

It would be virtually impossible to uncover how string instruments were first developed, but one can easily imagine that the idea was stumbled upon by some long-distant ancestor who noticed the pleasing sound produced by plucking a taut string, such as that found on a hunting bow. Ultimately it was discovered that strings make a sound not only when plucked, but also when tapped or rubbed. Even the wind can cause a string to vibrate, as occurs with the type of instrument called the Æolian harp.

Strings can be made from a wide variety of materials, including gut, silk, metal, plastic, animal hair, and all sorts of vegetable fibers. To produce an effective tone, though, a string is usually coupled to a hollow resonator (a soundbox) covered by some kind of flexible plate or membrane (a soundtable) that will amplify the vibrations. In many instances the soundtable is a thin panel of soft wood, preferably spruce which has experienced slow growth at a high altitude and therefore possesses a good combination of stiffness, lightness, and the abil-

fig. 23 (preceding page) **Detail from Giuseppe Maria Crespi,** (Bolognese), 1665–1747, *Woman Playing a Lute*, about 1700–05, oil on canvas, Charles Potter Kling Fund, 69.958

fig. 24 (above) **An East African musician posing with his bowl lyre**

ity to propagate soundwaves efficiently. One sees the application of a spruce soundtable in many familiar instruments, such as the violin and guitar. Throughout the world, however, many other types of timber, including hardwoods, are used for soundtables. Another alternative for a soundtable is a stretched membrane made from the skin of an animal or reptile. The banjo is a well-known instrument that employs such a membrane, which functions rather like the head of a drum. For the resonator or body to which a soundtable is attached, a wide variety of materials may be used, including woods, gourds, metals, and plastics. In most cases, though, the material is something fairly firm, since its main purpose is to provide a rigid structure and, in some instances, a hard surface that will reflect soundwaves away from the instrument. Maple is the preferred wood for the backs and sides of violins, for example.

String instruments show wonderful and appealing variety in their forms, from the pear-shaped body of the Renaissance lute and mandolin to the amazing diversity of "long zithers" and "spike fiddles" found throughout Asia – not to mention the vast array of shapes employed in twentieth-century guitars. Depending on the instrument maker's taste and the buyer's pocketbook, ornamentation can range from restrained elegance to exuberant excess. Carving, inlay, painting, and an endless number of recipes for stains and varnishes are all in the luthier's decorative arsenal.

fig. 25 **A Japanese musician playing a long zither (***koto***)**

Zither (*qin*)

China

Probably 17th century

With a history dating back three thousand years, the *qin* is highly esteemed in China, where it is considered a scholar's instrument, requiring deep concentration and meditation during playing. It also has the largest and oldest repertoire of any Chinese musical instrument. The seven silk strings of the *qin* are plucked with the fingernails of the right hand, while the left hand presses down the strings to select different notes. Although the *qin* was played as part of an ensemble at various times in its history, including official and ceremonial music at the court, it has come to be thought of as primarily a solo instrument.

Extensive symbolism and ideology surround the form, construction, dimensions, and performance of the *qin*. For example, the curved top is meant to symbolize heaven, while the flat bottom board represents earth. Man's presence, as the player, completes the philosophical ordering. The exact composition of the several coats of lacquer applied to the outer surfaces by its maker is generally kept a secret, further adding to the instrument's mystique. Some believe the age and authenticity of such instruments can be determined by examining the pattern of cracks that this lacquer takes on over time. The classic form of the *qin*, as seen in the instrument pictured here, was standardized by at least A.D. 200.

Like many old examples, this present *qin* bears various inscriptions on its underside, including one that provides its name, *Taigu yiyin*, which may be translated as "Tone of Antiquity." There is likewise an inscription implying that the instrument was constructed in 1233, although most scholars are convinced that it actually dates to the seventeenth century. Depiction of the *qin* in paintings and decorative arts of China is extremely common.

Wutong wood, zi wood
L. 121 cm, w. 19 cm, h. 11 cm
(L. 47 5/8 in., w. 7 1/2 in., h. 4 15/16 in.)
Gift of Jane E. Affelder in memory of Paul B. Affelder
1981.782

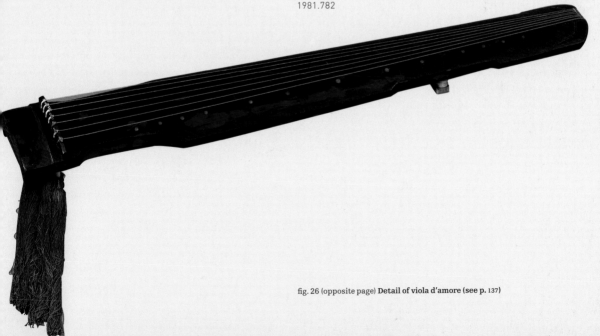

fig. 26 (opposite page) Detail of viola d'amore (see p. 137)

Zither (*mí-gyaùng*)
Burma
Mid-19th century

Zoomorphism is frequently encountered in ethno-graphic musical instruments, but rarely is the inter-pretation as compelling as with the *mí-gyaùng* (meaning "crocodile zither"). The Mon people in the southern region of Burma developed this type of instrument centuries ago. Such zithers are almost never played there today, however, and little is known about the *mí-gyaùng* except that it is related to the *chakhé* (also meaning "crocodile"), a zither of pres-ent-day Thailand. Like many other varieties of long zithers, the *mí-gyaùng* may have evolved from the *qin*, which would account for the high esteem in which such instruments are held as family heirlooms even today.

Tropical hardwood
L. 113.8 cm, w. 15.6 cm, h. 15.9 cm
(L. 44 ¹³/₁₆ in., w. 6 ⅛ in., h. 6 ¼ in.)
Arthur Tracy Cabot Fund   1993.11

Miniature zither (*koto*)
Japan
19th century

Long zithers are found among the cultures of most East Asian countries, though many of these instru-ments probably share their ancestry with Chinese prototypes such as the *qin*. Several different forms of long zither are played in Japan, but the most impor-tant one is the *koto*, which is further sub-divided in various types associated with particular musical genres. Since the sixteenth century, there have like-wise existed several schools of *koto* playing and repertoire. There is a long tradition of solo music for the *koto*, but the instrument is also featured as part of a trio ensemble that nowadays includes the *shamisen* (lute) and *shakuhachi* (end-blown flute). Since the middle of the last century, the *koto* has found many interested proponents in the West, some of whom have composed concertos for the instru-ment, accompanied by a symphony orchestra.

The *koto*'s thirteen silk strings are plucked with various shaped picks – made of bamboo, bone, or ivory – worn on the thumb, index, and middle finger of the right hand. The left hand damps the string vibrations and alters the pitch by pressing down on the strings beyond the bridges. A slight, ornamental inflection of the pitch is also executed in this manner. The bridges are movable, so by changing their place-ment one can change the instrument's tuning.

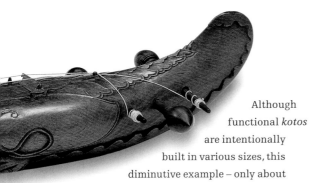

Although functional *kotos* are intentionally built in various sizes, this diminutive example – only about one-fifth as long as a full-size instrument – was apparently made only as a decorative piece. Even so, it reproduces all the technical features of a regular *koto*, and is skillfully lacquered along its sides with intricate landscape scenes. Several examples of small *kotos* like this are known. As keepsake objects, they were attractive to collectors, and have subsequently found their way into museums.

Kiri wood, ivory, lacquer
L. 53.8 cm, w. 11.2 cm, h. 8 cm
(L. 21 ³/₁₆ in., w. 4 ⁷/₁₆ in., h. 3 ⅛ in.)
Leslie Lindsey Mason Collection   17.2150

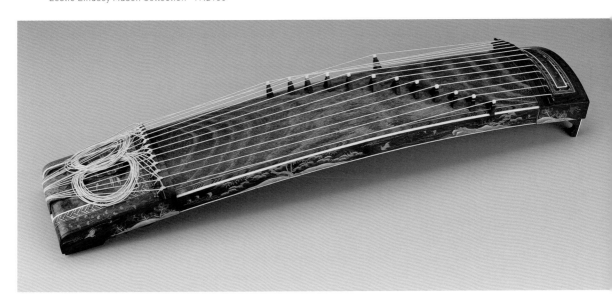

Zither (Appalachian dulcimer)
James Edward Thomas, about 1850–1933
United States (Bath, Kentucky)
1913

The so-called Appalachian dulcimer is not a true
dulcimer, which has strings struck with slender
mallets. Instead, it is a type of zither with frets, the
strings of which are plucked with a pick,
traditionally a feather quill. The instruments we now
recognize of this type were developed sometime in
the second half of the nineteenth century, based
primarily on a straight-sided German-style zither
called the *Scheitholt*. Other forms evolved from this
parent instrument, including one with outward-
curving sides that created a cigar shape. Until fairly
recently, scholars were unaware of these earlier
prototypes and assumed that the elongated,
hourglass shape with three strings was the norm.
But this style of instrument is, in fact, not firmly
documented until the early 1870s.

The first maker of such a dulcimer who is recorded
by name is James Edward Thomas of eastern Kentucky, known among his friends as "Uncle Ed."
Thomas was a prolific builder of dulcimers, though
like most makers of his time he worked in relative
isolation and with simple tools. He was also influential, teaching his craft to Jethro Amburgey of Hind-
man, Kentucky, who became one of the most noted

dulcimer makers of the next generation. With the
general revival of crafts in the early nineteenth
century, the construction of dulcimers became more
widespread. Handicraft organizations were gradually formed in various parts of the Appalachian
region, including the Southern Handicrafts Guild,
which has been especially influential in rekindling
interest in dulcimer making in post-war America.

The dulcimer shown here is an exceptionally well-
preserved and elegant example of Thomas's work.
It shows virtually no wear, and may have been
brought back to New England as a souvenir by one
of the many young female school teachers who were
assigned to the rural regions of Appalachia. Thomas
was once asked why he painted some of his instruments black, and his simple reply was that he
happened to have a can of black paint sitting around
his shop.

Walnut
L. 86.8 cm, w. 15.8 cm, h. 4.2 cm
(L. 34 3/16 in., w. 6 1/4 in., h. 1 5/8 in.)
Gift of Mrs. Edward Jackson Holmes 1989.129

Dulcimer (*yangqin*)
Workshop of Ji Xian
China (Guangzhou)
Probably late 19th century

A subdivision of the broader classification of string instruments called zithers, dulcimers are defined by the fact that their strings are struck rather than plucked. The name is derived from ancient Greek and Latin words, *dulce melos*, meaning "sweet sound." Dulcimers are found in many parts of the world, and their shape is usually that of a wide trapezoid. Case size, number of strings, and types of mallet all vary from country to country, and the instrument may be suspended from the player's neck with a strap, placed on a table or stand, or have its own legs. Strings are always arranged in groups of two or more (called courses), each tuned to the same unison note. Careful placement of the bridge at a position that creates a 2:3 ratio of a string's vibrating length will allow one side to sound a fifth higher than the other, thus creating two different pitches from one course of strings. Although mostly regarded as a folk instrument in Europe, an early eighteenth-century dulcimer virtuoso named Panteleon Hebenstreit so impressed Louis XIV with his playing that the king had the instrument renamed the *panteleon*, an appellation that remained in effect in some locales for most of a century.

There is no concrete evidence to ascribe the dulcimer's origins specifically to Persia, as has often been done, though the instrument does hold a distinguished place in classical Iranian music. Its actual birthplace was probably somewhere along the eastern edge of the Mediterranean Sea, from whence it was transplanted to Europe and East Asia, perhaps to the latter region via Jesuit missionaries. In Mandarin Chinese, the instrument's name, *yangqin*, translates as "foreign stringed instrument," perhaps because it utilizes wire strings rather than the silk strings traditional to the Far East. Although the dulcimer is a relative newcomer to Chinese music, it has readily been incorporated into instrumental ensembles. The undamped ringing of the *yanqin*'s thin metal strings is an unmistakable sound, as is the rapid two-hand tremolo that colors much of the instrument's music. The beaters used to strike the strings are very slender and springy slats of bamboo. A tuning hammer for the instrument can be safely stored in a narrow drawer mounted in the front part of the case.

Paulownia, other woods, ivory
L. 70 cm, w. 25 cm, h. 11 cm
(L. 27 9/16 in., w. 9 13/16 in., h. 4 5/16 in.)
Leslie Lindsey Mason Collection   17.2064

Psaltery (*kantele*)

Finland

19th century

The psaltery is a variety of zither in which open-tuned strings are plucked, but generally not pressed against a fingerboard or other surface to change their pitch. Psalteries similar to the *kantele* are found throughout the region of the eastern Baltic Sea, although it is most strongly associated with Finland, where, as the country's oldest folk instrument, it serves as a strong national symbol. The mythical creation of the *kantele* was first described in the ancient, epic poem *Kalevala*, where the sage Väinämöinen constructed one from the jawbone of a pike and the hair of a maiden. There are various versions of the story, one of which says that the strings were made from the hair of a horse belonging to a demon called Hisii. In another rendition, Väinämöinen loses his first *kantele* in the sea, and the tears he sheds over its loss turn into amber. He then makes a second *kantele* from a birch tree, with a sound so beautiful that animals are charmed by it, quite like Orpheus and his lyre.

The earliest known *kantele*s can be dated only to the eighteenth century. This particular example is constructed in the old manner, with its body hollowed out from a solid block of birch and the top covered by a thin pine soundboard. Later instruments were made from separate pieces of wood constituting the back, sides, and top. Väinämöinen's instrument was described as having five strings, and five-string *kantele*s were still being played in the early 1800s. But like many musical instruments, performers sought to improve and enlarge it, adding more strings, which were probably at an early date changed to ones made of gut and eventually metal wire. The strings are sometimes plucked with the fingertips of both hands, but can also be strummed with the fingers or a pick.

As recently as the first half of the twentieth century, the *kantele* was so ubiquitous in Finland that it was considered customary for every man to own one. Its repertoire consists mainly of traditional folk songs, dances, and marches, which would work well with the limited number of notes available on simpler models. There are now *kantele*s that are completely chromatic, however, and enough interest has been maintained in the instrument in modern times that contemporary pieces have been composed specifically for it.

Birch, pine
L. 69.5 cm, w. 21.7 cm, h. 7.2 cm
(L. 27 3/8 in., w. 8 9/16 in., h. 2 13/16 in.)
Leslie Lindsey Mason Collection   17.1771

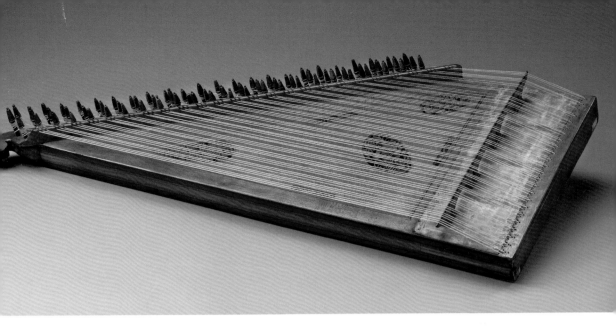

Psaltery (*kanun*)

Turkey

19th century

Although it is seldom mentioned in writings earlier than the nineteenth century, the *kanun* may have its roots in Egypt far earlier. There is evidence that archaic examples were held vertically and played only with the right hand, but modern versions are always placed horizontally on a table or the player's lap. A thin soundtable of sheepskin stretched laterally across an open portion of the wide end of the body serves to amplify three to four octaves of gut strings, which are plucked with ring-shaped picks placed on the index fingers of both hands. On a modern *kanun* the strings are metal and their pitch can be finely adjusted with rotating brass levers, allowing the player to easily create a wide range of tunings, with subtle variations as to the exact pitches.

The *kanun*, or *gānūn*, is one of the most admired and sophisticated instruments of classical music in Turkey and the Arab world. Considered an aristocratic instrument, it is heard primarily in urban areas, and is taught in music conservatories throughout much of the Middle East. Although a solo instrument, it is almost always heard in traditional orches-tras of the region, where it holds a principal position. To accommodate greater virtuosity by its players, the *kanun* has grown in size and number of strings since its introduction in the early 1800s. There is considerable interest in maintaining and renewing the traditions of *kanun* playing in the present day, with several performers having risen to prominence.

The strings of this nineteenth-century *kanun* are placed in groups of three, which is a fairly typical arrangement. There are no tuning levers. Instead, pyramid-shaped wood tuning pegs are adjusted with a specially shaped wrench. Carved into the sound-holes are foliate decorations in a Persian motif called the "leaf of life," which suggests that the *kanun*'s distribution may, at times, have extended into parts of South Asia.

Walnut, sheepskin

L. 92.3 cm, w. 38 cm, h. 5 cm

(L. 36 ⁵⁄₁₆ in., w. 14 ¹⁵⁄₁₆ in., h. 1 ¹⁵⁄₁₆ in.)

Leslie Lindsey Mason Collection   17.1772

Double psaltery (*spitzharfe*)

Germany

About 1670

Extremely little has been written about the *spitzharfe* (literally "pointed harp"), apart from its brief mention in two German musical treatises published in the 1730s. Based on the few surviving examples that were signed by their makers, the instrument appears to have originated in either Germany or Scandinavia, and was popular in Northern Europe only for a short time between about 1690 and 1750. Also called the *arpanetta*, the instrument is not actually a harp at all, but rather a type of psaltery with strings on both sides of its soundbox.

Although there are no historical depictions of a *spitzharfe* being played, it was designed to be set upright on a table or on the performer's lap and plucked with the fingernails, the shortest strings placed nearer to the player, as with a conventional harp. The right hand plays the melody on iron strings, while the left hand provides a bass accompaniment, usually on strings of brass or other copper alloy. It appears that no music was ever specifically composed for the *spitzharfe*. Instead, the genteel amateurs who played the instrument probably adapted simple two-part songs and dances.

Most surviving *spitzharfen* are nicely decorated in a manner akin to that of harpsichords and other domestic keyboard instruments of the period. The ornamentation of the MFA's instrument is fairly typical, with birds, flowers, and cupids painted on both of the soundboards, along with delicate rosettes made of parchment. The sides of the case are colored to imitate the black and red mottling of tortoiseshell, and the long, straight side contains a small portrait of a lady, set in a diamond-shaped wooden frame. The top of some *spitzharfen* is carved with the head of an animal (often a lion), although this particular one terminates in a large scroll.

Spruce

H. 116 cm, w. 38.4 cm, d. 8.4 cm

(H. 45 ¹¹⁄₁₆ in., w. 15 ⅛ in., d. 3 ⁵⁄₁₆ in.)

Leslie Lindsey Mason Collection   17.1773

Bowl lyre (*ndongo*)

Ganda people

Uganda

19th century

The lyre is one of most ancient forms of stringed musical instruments, its creation first described in a Homeric hymn to Hermes. It is almost only in eastern Africa, however, that lyres have continued to be made and played in modern times. Several different styles of lyre are known in Uganda, but the *ndongo* is perhaps the best known. It is classified as a bowl lyre, since its round body is hollowed out like a bowl and then covered with the skin of a monitor lizard, which serves as a soundtable. This use of reptile skin is the instrument's most unique feature, and is found on only one other type of lyre. As the *ndongo* has no bridge to lift its strings from the surface of the soundtable, they vibrate against the rough, scaly surface of the lizard-skin covering, creating a very distinctive buzzing tone. Regrettably, the monitor lizard is now an endangered species, making it virtually impossible to construct an *ndongo* in the traditional manner. Tassels of goat hair or cow's tails always adorn the ends of the wooden yoke that carries the strings. Without them, the joint between the yoke and the supporting arms would look unduly "naked," to quote one contemporary *ndongo* player.

The *ndongo* is often used as part of an ensemble of fiddle, flute, and drum, but its more significant capacity is to accompany a solo singer whose songs serve three important roles in Ugandan culture: teaching moral conduct, storytelling, and initiating a newlywed couple on their wedding night. In each of these practices the performer's playing is largely improvised and involves complex rhythmic patterns played in a very rapid and percussive style, despite the presence of only eight strings tuned in a pentatonic scale.

Unlike European harps, whose notes are strung sequentially from low to high, the lowest strings of the *ndongo* are in the middle and the higher ones to both sides. The same arrangement of notes is found on other African instruments such as the harp-lute (*kora*) and the lamellaphone (thumb piano). The *ndongo*'s strings are wrapped around its yoke with a tuning loop that provides enough friction to allow their pitch to be changed by twisting them around this wooden rod. Unless it is being played with other instruments, the *ndongo* is simply tuned to suit the performer's singing voice for a particular piece.

Wood, monitor lizard skin, goat hair, seashells
H. 66 cm, w. 53.5 cm, d. 10.5 cm
(H. 26 in., w. 21 1/16 in., d. 4 1/8 in.)
Leslie Lindsey Mason Collection   17.2179

Arched harp (*kundi*)
Mangbetu people
Democratic Republic of Congo
Late 19th century

A greater variety of harps is found in sub-Saharan Africa than anywhere else in the world. Unlike European harps, however, they do not have a triangular framework. They instead assume an arched or sometimes angled form in which the slender neck curves away from the body, with no front pillar supporting the free end of the neck. The hollow body, usually carved from a solid block of wood, is covered on top with animal skin, or occasionally that of a reptile. Depending on the harp's regional origins, the body itself may be constructed in one of several shapes, including ovoid, hemispherical, boat, and waisted. The tradition of arched harps stretches back over five thousand years, although it is uncertain whether they might have been transferred to Africa from Egypt and the Near East or vice versa. The strings of African harps are traditionally made from twisted animal tendons or vegetable fibers, but as with so many other ethnographic string instruments, performers are now using more durable nylon, often in the form of commercially available fishing line.

Arched harps may have as few as four strings or as many as ten, but five is common. Playing position also varies from type to type and region to region; the neck may be placed away from the performer, pressed against the chest, or positioned at some angle in between. African harpists mostly use the instrument to accompany their own voice, and many of them are highly respected specialists in the art of composing praise songs honoring important people or narratives of heroic prowess. Harps are also occasionally played in ensemble with other harps or instruments.

Arched harps from Africa's Congo region are especially prized among collectors, as they exhibit particularly attractive shapes and carving. Some are remarkably anthropomorphic in appearance (especially among the Ngbaka people of the Ubangi region), with two carved legs extending from the lower end of the body and supporting the instrument like a statue when displayed. This rather petite *kundi* is made in a form commonly used for Mangbetu harps, with a tightly waisted body and two round soundholes piercing the soundtable at opposite corners. Like most harps from central Africa, its gracefully curved neck terminates in a carved head. With white beads serving as eyes, the head itself is elegantly elongated, a shape considered beautiful among the Mangbetu people, achieved by intentionally reshaping their skulls and accentuating them with a tall coiffure.

Wood, cowhide
L. 57 cm, w. 14.5 cm, d. 6 cm
(L. 22⁷⁄₁₆ in., w. 5¹¹⁄₁₆ in., d. 2⅜ in.)
Helen and Alice Colburn Fund and William E. Nickerson Fund   1994.194

Harp (*clàirseach*)
John Kelly, working 1726–1734
Ireland (Baltdaniel)
1734

The harp is a national symbol in Ireland, where it has a long and honorable history dating back to the twelfth century. Unique among European harps, the *clàirseach* had brass strings rather than gut and was often plucked with long, pointed fingernails rather than fingertips, producing a bright and resonant tone. In Medieval and early Renaissance times, such harps were small (about twenty-eight inches high) and played resting on the performer's lap. Irish harpers were held in high esteem during this period, and their primary role was to accompany the recitation of bardic poetry. Regard for harping gradually eroded, however, and performers were often left struggling to make ends meet.

Over time, Irish harps also gradually grew in size, resulting in the type of large, high-headed model shown here. As inscribed on its front pillar, it was made for Reverend Charles Bunworth, a great musical patron who helped preserve the dying tradition of Irish harp playing during the eighteenth century. Bunworth also collected old Irish harps, and in a tragic turn of affairs many of them were burned as firewood by his servants during one of the family's absences from home. Only about a dozen Irish harps built before 1800 are known to survive today, and this is the only example located outside the British Isles. It is also one of the only musical instruments in the MFA's collection whose history can be traced all the way back to its original owner.

Bog oak
H. 169 cm, w. 79 cm, d. 34.5 cm
(H. 66 ⁹⁄₁₆ in., w. 31 ⅛ in., d. 13 ⁹⁄₁₆ in.)
Leslie Lindsey Mason Collection   17.1787

Pedal harp

Godefroi Holtzman, working 1780–1794

France (Paris)

About 1785

The earliest European harps were designed to be tuned only to a diatonic scale (the equivalent of the "white notes" on a piano), and so various solutions were gradually attempted to furnish the accidental notes. One means, in use in Italy by the sixteenth century, was to provide an additional row of strings that could be tuned to the sharps and flats. A similar concept, using three rows of strings, was later implemented in Wales. By the late seventeenth century, German harp makers were placing metal levers near the upper ends of the strings, which could be turned against the strings to shorten their sounding length and thereby raise their pitch one half step. These levers had to be operated by hand, and the system was consequently rather cumbersome. Connecting the operation of these levers to a foot-activated pedal was the next logical step in the harp's development.

Pedal harps were first manufactured in Germany about 1720, and by the 1770s had become quite popular, especially in France. Pressing on one of the seven pedals simultaneously raises the pitch of certain strings by half a musical tone, thus providing the player with the ability to produce a complete chromatic scale. Such a mechanism is called a "single action," and was used on harps well into the 1800s. A more advanced mechanism, called the "double action," allowed a player to further depress the pedal to a second position, thus raising the pitch of some strings a full musical step when needed. This double action, patented in 1810 in Paris by Sébastien Érard, remains in use on today's concert harps. French makers firmly dominated the design and manufacture of pedal harps for more than a century, until two Chicago firms began to offer similar models beginning in the late 1800s.

The graceful outline of harps lends itself to carved and painted decoration, which here includes bucolic scenes on the soundboard and Chinese-inspired

designs on both sides of the curved neck. With their elegant sound and appearance, pedal harps were an appealing instrument for women in courtly circles. Marie Antoinette played the harp – the ownership of countless instruments has been ascribed to her – and so, of course, did many women who hoped to emulate her. Several composers of the Classical era began to exploit the musical possibilities of the new pedal harp, including Mozart, who in 1778 wrote a much-loved concerto for harp and flute.

Maple, spruce

H. 157.5 cm, w. 72 cm, d. 35.5 cm

(H. 62 in., w. 28⅜ in., d.14 in.)

Leslie Lindsey Mason Collection 18.30

Lute (*rubāb*)

Afghanistan

About 1950

The *rubāb* is the national instrument of Afghanistan, played by amateurs and professionals alike for both popular and serious music. It is used predominantly by male performers in small ensembles that accompany the voice, and for a limited but distinctive solo repertoire that was probably composed at the Afghan court during the late nineteenth century. Similarly shaped lutes are distributed throughout Pakistan, the Kashmir region, and northern India, where they have assumed a larger form called the *sarod*, with a polished metal fingerboard. The Afghan version is not particularly ancient, and was probably devised sometime during the eighteenth century.

The tightly waisted body and neck of the *rubāb* are carved from one piece of mulberry wood, with a thin piece of goatskin glued over the lower half of the body to serve as a soundtable. A number of small soundholes pierce this skin, as well as the lower end of the fingerboard. The three main strings, usually tuned in fourths, are made from gut and plucked with a small wooden pick. A *rubāb* may additionally have three to four drone strings and as many as fifteen sympathetic strings of metal wire that are tuned to the modal scale of the music being performed. Although the sympathetic strings are present primarily to reinforce the tone of the main strings, they are sometimes struck individually as well. Smaller sizes of *rubāb* are used for regional music of the Pashtun people, while larger ones are generally reserved for performance of classical compositions.

An interesting tradition of musical performance in parts of Afghanistan is its combination with birdsong, which is considered the highest expression of musical aesthetic. It was believed that birds were encouraged to sing by the sound of music, and that the more they responded, the better the music was. To that end, caged birds were often intentionally brought to performances to enhance the overall experience.

Mulberry wood, goatskin
L. 74.8 cm, w. 14.4 cm, d. 17.5 cm
(L. 29 7/16 in., w. 5 11/16 in., d. 6 7/8 in.)
Gift of Joseph R. Coolidge
in memory of his wife,
Peggy Stuart Coolidge   1981.773

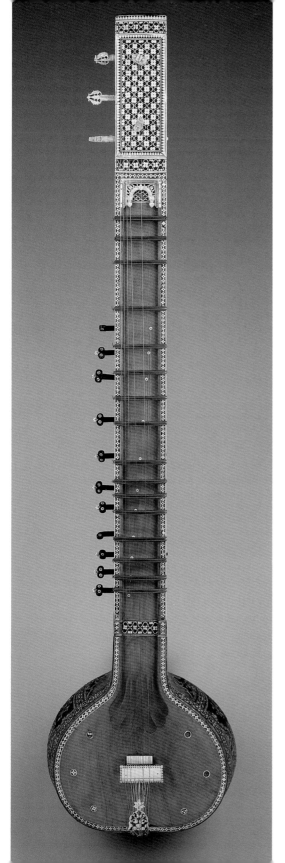

Lute (sitar)

India (possibly Bikaner, Rajasthan)

Early 20th century

Certainly the most emblematic instrument of northern India and surrounding regions, the sitar dates back to the thirteenth century. The name comes from an old Persian word *sihtār*, meaning "three-stringed," which indicates the musical resources of the very earliest instruments. The modern form of sitar dates to the period of the late Mughal empire (1707–1858), and continues to be refined to this day. The main strings (lying over the curved brass frets) are plucked with a wire pick on the right index finger and fretted with the left middle and index fingers, which can pull the strings sideways to alter the pitch interval as much as a fifth. The numerous sympathetic strings (lying below the frets) are not played, but vibrate in resonance with the main strings. In music of the classical style the sitar is normally accompanied by another string instrument of somewhat similar shape called a *tambūrā*, which provides a drone, and a pair of drums called *tablā*.

This sitar is of quite delicate design compared with modern instruments, and particularly refined in its decoration. The hollow calabash gourd that constitutes the body is covered with elaborate, gold-colored floral designs, while the edges of the body and neck and the face of the headstock are inlaid with an intricate mosaic made from pieces of ivory set into black mastic. The ivory tuning pegs for the main strings are especially beautiful, each carved with two birds standing back to back.

Toonwood, calabash gourd, ivory
L. 118 cm, w. 28 cm, d. 22 cm
(L. 46 7/16 in., w. 11 in., d. 8 11/16 in.)
Bequest of Estate of Mrs. Dona Luisa Coomaraswamy
1971.84

Lute (*sarasvatī vīṇā*)

India (southern region)

About 1850–75

The *vīṇā* is the most prominent string instrument of south Indian classical music. It is often referred to specifically as the *sarasvatī vīṇā*, since according to mythology it symbolizes the body of the Hindu goddess of learning and music, Sarasvatī (the frets, for example, represent her ribs). Likewise, certain parts of the instrument are related to the various chakras or psychic centers of yoga. Played mainly by members of the elite upper class, the *vīṇā* is usually employed only in a cultivated, art-music tradition. Important schools of performance were developed at the local courts of the rajas prior to the eighteenth century, although modern playing has become influenced by music of north India.

The rounded body and hollow neck of this *vīṇā* are carved from one solid piece of jackfruit wood, indicating that it is a high-quality instrument. Attached below the neck is a large calabash gourd, which provides additional resonance. Surmounting the pegbox is a carved dragon (*yāli*), a traditional feature of the

sarasvatī vīṇā, and a symbol of power and protection. The fingerboard's brass frets are held in place with a matrix of blackened wax, deeply scalloped between each fret. This scalloping allows the player maximum freedom to press and pull the strings, producing the various glides and ornaments that are an integral part of its music. The sustained, nasal sound of the *vīṇā* is rich in harmonics, a characteristic of other Indian musical instruments. As in the sitar, for example, this effect is produced by carefully shaping the top of the instrument's tablelike bridge, creating a parabolic curve that causes the strings to vibrate against this surface in a particular way to create the desired tone.

Jackfruit wood, calabash gourd, ivory
L. 110 cm, w. 29 cm, d. 30 cm
(L. 43 5/16 in., w. 11 7/16 in., d. 11 13/16 in.)
Edwin E. Jack Fund   1995.86

Lute (*pipa*)

China

1891

Developed from an instrument originating in Central Asia before the fourth century, the *pipa* gradually became an important element of Chinese musical culture, providing a principal entertainment for banquets at court. Some have suggested that its name is onomatopoeic for the sound made by plucking the strings to-and-fro, while others trace these two syllables to terms that indicate the actual motion of the hand in this process. Repertoire for the *pipa*, mostly transmitted by oral tradition, is divided into "civil" and "martial" pieces. Refined and graceful in nature, the former are considered feminine. Conversely, martial pieces are understandably masculine and more powerful, and are likewise played faster and louder.

Up until the Tang dynasty (618–907), the four strings of the *pipa* were made of silk and played with a single pick, but since then performers have used their fingernails or small picks placed on their fingertips. The modern-day *pipa* has steel strings, which creates considerably greater projection and volume. There has also been a gradual increase in the number of frets, which on today's instruments allow for a range of three octaves. These frets rise quite high from the fingerboard so that the player can bend notes by depressing the strings, unlike the sideways motion used for a similar effect by Western performers on the guitar. The *pipa* is also held in a much more vertical position than the guitar, with the tuning pegs near the player's left ear. Almost all present-day players of the *pipa* are female: as young men have begun pursuing other interests, like computers, it has gradually become more acceptable for women to perform music professionally.

The pear-shaped body of the *pipa* is relatively shallow, the one-piece back hollowed out from various hardwoods, including teak. Like most other plucked string instruments of China, the belly or

soundboard is traditionally made from wutong wood, a lightweight and resonant material. The peg-box is almost always surmounted by some carved design, which may abstractly represent objects such as a flower, dragon's head, or bat. On the instrument shown here, this form appears to be the stylized tail of a phoenix. Ivory plaques on the fingerboard are incised with poetic couplets that have been partially translated as "dreaming while boating in the Southern skies, with no clouds visible."

Teak, wutong, ivory
L. 99.3 cm, w. 30.5 cm, d. 5.5 cm
(L. 39 ⅛ in., w. 12 in., d. 2 ⅛ in.)
Leslie Lindsey Mason Collection   17.2049

Lute (*shamisen*)

Japan

Before 1820

Since the seventeenth century, the *shamisen* has been used for music enjoyed by many levels of Japanese society, from folk and theatrical forms to art music. It usually accompanies a singer, and instruments of varying size are employed for different types of music. To some, it will be most familiar as the primary accompaniment for *Bunraku* puppet theater. The thin edge of a large, triangular pick (*bachi*) produces a sharp sound as it strikes the string and thin skin head simultaneously. Somewhat disconcerting to pet owners of the Western world, the preferred membrane material for covering the front and back of a *shamisen*'s wood body is dog or cat skin, the latter considered the best.

Historically, the *shamisen* is related to a Chinese instrument called the *sanxian* (meaning "three strings"), the oval body of which is covered with snakeskin. Tradition holds that the first instrument akin to the *shamisen* was introduced into Japan about 1562 from the Ryukyu Islands, and at that time still resembled the Chinese *sanxian* in most respects. Japanese players of a lute called the *biwa*, however, sought to improve the instrument, discovering that a preferable tone could be produced with a larger pick and by changing the material of the soundtable to cat skin. On the inside surfaces of the four wood pieces that constitute a modern *shamisen* body, the maker carves herringbone patterns that are said to greatly improve the instrument's tone quality.

The craftsmanship of this particular *shamisen* is of very high quality throughout, from the slender, shapely neck to the intricate landscape scenes lacquered on the sides of the body. More highly decorated than is typical, it was probably used in refined settings for private entertainment, and must have been highly prized by its previous owners. Inscriptions on the instrument's storage case indicate that in 1820 it was owned by Matsudaira, the Lord of Shinamo in the area called Nanbu. The instrument itself may well be older.

Persimmon, shitan, cat skin
L. 96 cm, w. 19 cm, d. 8.8 cm
(L. 37 13/16 in., w. 7 1/2 in., d. 3 7/16 in.)
Frederick Brown Fund and William Lindsey Fund by exchange   1992.62

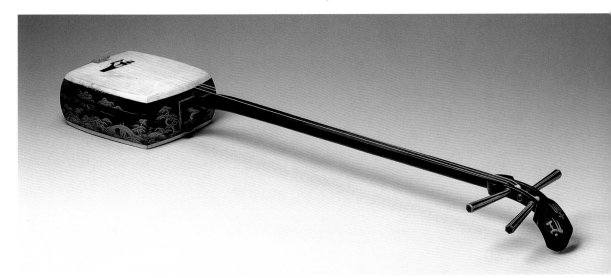

Lute (*charango*)

Peru

19th century

The *charango* is one of various guitarlike instruments found throughout Latin America that were created by indigenous peoples in the wake of European contact. Distinctive features were adopted for many of these instruments, but the diminutive *charango* is particularly unusual, with a curved back often made from the shell of the *quirqincho*, a relative of the armadillo. It has been said that the soul of the animal is kept alive by playing such an instrument. Modern *charangos* are more typically made entirely from wood, as *quirqincho* shells tend to warp with age and do not provide as good a resonance. The highly portable *charango* is found in modern-day Peru, Boliva, Ecuador, and parts of northern Chile and Argentina. Cradled in the musician's arms and variously strummed or plucked with the middle finger, it may be played alone – in a style more akin to flamenco guitar than classical – or combined with Andean flutes, panpipes, drums, and rattles. One researcher has related the instrument's name to words in the local Quechua language that mean "noisy" and "joyful."

Quirqincho shell, wood
L. 56 cm, w. 13.9 cm, d. 7.9 cm
(L. 22 ¹/₁₆ in., w. 5 ½ in., d. 3 ⅛ in.)
Leslie Lindsey Mason Collection   17.2241

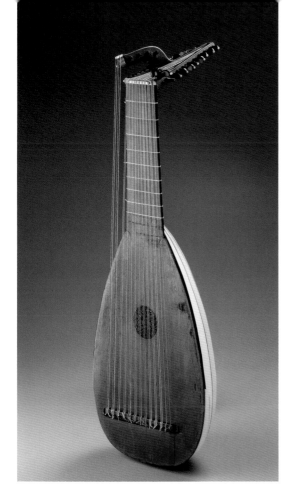

Lute

Andreas Berr, 1650–1722

Austria (Vienna)

1699

It was from contact with Arab civilizations that Europe first acquired the lute toward the end of the thirteenth century. Although its pear-shaped body remained essentially the same, the instrument was gradually transformed into one with a wider neck that carried six pairs of strings rather than four single strings, and was played with the fingertips rather than a quill or pick. Depicted in countless paintings and other works of art, the lute was by far Europe's most highly regarded musical instrument during the sixteenth and seventeenth centuries. Its gentle, soothing sound, charming by itself, blends very well with other instruments and the human voice.

Much of the reason for the lute's highly responsive tone is its remarkably delicate construction. The curved ribs that make up the back are often no thicker than a millimeter, and the spruce soundboard is similarly thin in order for it to be as acoustically sensitive as possible. Given its feather-light body, the pegbox that extends from the end of the lute's neck must be bent back at a steep angle in order to help keep the balance point closer to the center. Because of their fragile construction, lutes have suffered an extremely low rate of survival. Add to that the myriad alterations that historical examples have undergone over the past three centuries, and we are left with only a handful of instruments that reflect their original condition. Countless fakes also cloud the picture, but they are generally easy to spot because of their clumsy and overly heavy construction. A fine lute will practically tremble in the player's hands, allowing performance of music that is at once intricate and expressive.

This elegant ivory lute dates from the instrument's final years of popularity in German-speaking countries during the early eighteenth century, when composers such as Silvius Leopold Weiss and Johann Sebastian Bach created some of its most demanding solo repertoire. Lutes with ivory backs are not especially common, and were usually owned by aristocratic players. Little is recorded about Andreas Berr, this instrument's maker, and only one other lute from his shop is known to survive. But a 1727 performance treatise by composer and lutenist Ernst Gottlieb Baron highly commends his instruments.

Ivory, ebony, spruce
L. 81 cm, w. 28.3 cm, d. 13.5 cm
(L. 31⅞ in., w. 11⅛ in., d. 5⁵⁄₁₆ in.)
Arthur T. Cabot Fund   1986.7

Guitar

Jacopo Checchucci, dates unknown
Italy (Livorno)
1628

Guitars with five pairs of strings, rather than the six singles present on modern guitars, were in use by at least the late fifteenth century, and this arrangement of strings remained the norm throughout the Baroque period and up through the late 1700s. During this time guitars also had frets that were not permanently fixed to the fingerboard, but were instead made of tied-on gut, the same material used for the strings. Many of the earliest surviving guitars were made in Italy and are elaborately embellished, like this example.

As is common in early guitars, the back of this instrument is vaulted rather than flat, constructed from seventeen curved staves of ebony over a substrate of soft wood. The decoration is particularly elaborate, with scrolling ivory inlay on the back and sides and delicate arabesques of black mastic set into the spruce top. An especially fine rosette is set into the soundhole, constructed from thin pieces of gilded parchment. Although this curious and delicate structure affects the instrument's tone slightly, its main purpose was to adorn what would otherwise be a large gaping hole in an object that is almost completely covered with ornamentation.

Someone of considerable wealth and status was certainly the original owner of this visually stunning object. This is corroborated by the incorporation of a double-headed eagle into the decoration, a heraldic device for the Austrian House of Hapsburg. Unfortunately, nothing is known of this guitar's maker, Jacopo Checchucci, but the style of ornamentation is similar to that on guitars and lutes made in Venice during the same period by members of the Sellas family, several of whose instruments have been preserved.

Because of their relative fragility, remarkably few of the very earliest guitars have survived. Only about

Lyre guitar
Pons fils
France (Paris), 1810

thirty such instruments predating 1650 have been documented in museum collections, among which only two or three were made before 1600. Small-bodied guitars of the Baroque type also eventually went out of fashion, and many were undoubtedly discarded once they had outlived their usefulness. This would have been especially true of plainer instruments, leaving us today, for the most part, with only the most elaborate examples.

Ebony, ivory, spruce
L. 90 cm, w. 25.5 cm, d. 12 cm
(L 35 ⅞ in., w. 10 ⅙ in., d. 4 ¾ in.)
Museum purchase with funds donated anonymously;
Frank B. Bemis Fund; Morris and Louise Rosenthal Fund;
Frank T. Gangi, Global NAPs; Elizabeth Marie Paramino
Fund in memory of John F. Paramino, Boston Sculptor;
Jane Marsland and Judith A. Marsland Fund;
Mrs. Ralph P. Rudnick; and by exchange from Gift of
Joseph R. Coolidge in memory of his wife, Peggy Stuart
Coolidge; Gift of Mrs. Eleanor H. Wicher; Gift of Mrs. Ruth P.
Chase; and Gift of Dr. and Mrs. Vincent Pattavina 2001.707

Artists have been adapting the architectural and sculptural forms of ancient Greece and Rome into their work since the Renaissance. Fascination with artifacts of the classical world became especially strong in the late eighteenth and early nineteenth centuries, as many important archeological and artistic works from antiquity were rediscovered. The design and ornamentation of musical instruments was not exempt from this fad, as pianos and harps were dressed up with motifs borrowed from classical civilization.

The shape of this guitar is a direct result of that interest, emulating the form of the ancient Greek lyre. With a differently shaped sound cavity than the normal guitar, lyre guitars were meant to produce a deeper and slightly louder tone, but the result is also rather dull in color. Lyre guitars were made in many parts of Europe, but they were most popular in France. Most French lyre guitars of the early nineteenth century have slender, curved arms extending upward from the body, but this very ornate example evinces a more architectural approach, with stately wood columns supporting a gilded yoke terminating in exuberant spirals. This particular form is no more practical than any other style of lyre guitar, but its appearance would have greatly enhanced its appeal as interior decoration. As such, it is made with a flat bottom, like most lyre guitars, so that when not in use it could have been displayed as a proud indication of its owner's social status and regard for music.

Lyre guitars also provided an attractive fashion accessory for affluent young women, who might pose with the instrument for a painted portrait, dressed in a costume modeled after that of an ancient Greek musician. When actually trying to play such a clumsy guitar, though, her posture would have been far from graceful. In an age when personal decorum was supremely important among well-bred debutantes, this may have contributed to the relatively brief fashion for lyre guitars.

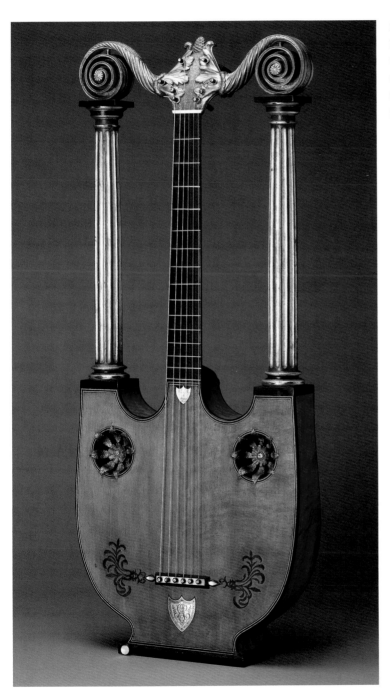

Satinwood, spruce, mahogany, ebony
L. 87.5 cm, w. 45.8 cm, d. 9.6 cm
(L. 3⅞/₁₆ in., w. 18 ¹/₁₆ in., d. 3 ¾ in.)
Museum purchase with funds donated
by Bradford M. and Dorothea R. Endicott
2000.972

Keyed English guitar (cittern)

Sold by Longman and Broderip

England (London)

1798

Part of a family of instruments called citterns, the eighteenth-century "English guitar" with metal strings and pear-shaped body was so called to differentiate it from the "Spanish guitar" with gut strings and waisted body. Relatively easy to play, English guitars were sometimes kept in barbershops for waiting clients to amuse themselves. They were also popular with upper-class ladies, and are often depicted in period portraiture, such as Thomas Gainsborough's well-known painting of the performer Ann Ford. There is a story about how one prominent English maker of harpsichords became annoyed that so many members of his female clientele were taking an interest in the English guitar, depriving him of instrument sales. As a recourse, he bought several cheap citterns and gave them out to milliners and other working-class women to bring shame upon the instrument, thus luring self-respecting ladies back to the more aristocratic harpsichord.

This particular instrument is exceptionally decorated, with green leaves hand-painted around the edge of the body, a solid ivory fingerboard, and an intricately carved ivory disk covering the soundhole, which incorporates what are probably the original owner's initials, ARL. It also contains an interesting feature sometimes added to English guitars, which is a set of six piano-style keys that propel small, leather-tipped hammers through the soundhole to strike the strings. Such a mechanism allowed less-talented performers more immediate results with the instrument and avoided potential damage to the fingernails of female players.

Maple, spruce, ivory

L. 69.5 cm, w. 30.5 cm, d. 8.6 cm

(L. 27 ⅜ in., w. 12 in., d. 3 ⅜ in.)

Samuel Putnam Avery Fund   1999.1

Balalaika
Russia
19th century

One of the most popular folk instruments of Russia, the balalaika was originally a peasant's instrument, although Peter the Great employed balalaikas in a grand orchestral procession in 1715. Early balalaikas, like this small treble instrument, had gut strings and a relatively soft sound. But beginning in the 1880s, the balalaika was transformed into a more artistic instrument, built in a family of six sizes from contrabass to piccolo, and eventually fitted with metal strings. Composers as renowned as Tchaikovsky were impressed with the instrument, remarking on its lovely sound and the "striking effect it makes in the orchestra."

The delicate sound of a single balalaika often accompanies song and dance, but large ensembles are also common in Russia and elsewhere. Entire orchestras of balalaikas began making concert tours in the early 1900s, and similar ensembles were subsequently founded in England and the United States. The instrument found many new aficionados in the wake of the 1969 movie *Dr. Zhivago*, in which the film score's love theme is hauntingly rendered on a balalaika.

Spruce, pine
L. 63 cm, w. 31.2 cm, d. 8.1 cm
(L. 24 ¹³⁄₁₆ in., w. 12 ⁵⁄₁₆ in., d. 3 ³⁄₁₆ in.)
Leslie Lindsey Mason Collection   17.1750

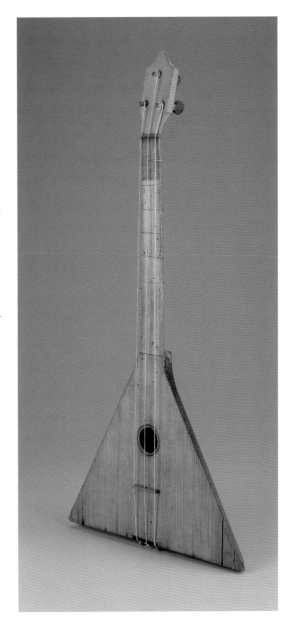

Banjo

Fairbanks and Company
United States (Boston, Massachusetts)
About 1904

Recorded observations from the late eighteenth
century describe American plantation slaves playing
a simple stringed instrument variously referred to
as the *banza* or *banjer*, with a gourd body over which
was stretched a tanned skin as a resonating membrane. These instruments were modeled after West
African prototypes formerly used by the slaves.
By the 1840s, the first true banjos evolved, with hoop-
shaped wood bodies covered by a calfskin membrane.
In the late nineteenth century, the banjo reached a
peak of popularity and was played even in performances of classical music. Boston was the most noted
center for high-quality banjo manufacture during
this period, and among the four manufacturers active
in the city, A. C. Fairbanks and Company made the
instruments most sought-after by players and collectors alike.

   This particular banjo is a fancy example of Fairbanks and Company's "Whyte-Laydie," their best
model. It was so-named because its neck is of light-
colored maple rather than the more common
mahogany used at the time. The engraving of the
mother-of-pearl inlay on the fingerboard is of notice-
ably finer quality than on most instruments of the
period, and the headstock is adorned with a characteristic example of what is usually referred to as a
griffin. The nickel silver rim that encases the circular
body incorporates a technical feature called a tone
ring, which enhances the sound and volume.

Maple, nickel silver, pearl, calfskin
L. 95 cm, w. 30.3 cm, d. 6.7 cm
(L. 37⅜ in., w. 11¹⁵⁄₁₆ in., d. 2⅝ in.)
Foster Charitable Fund   1997.64

Resonator guitar (Tri-cone model)
National String Instrument Corporation
United States (Los Angeles, California)
1934

The Slovakian-born Dopyera family working in Los
Angeles was the first to successfully develop a
"resophonic" guitar, which used shallow discs of spun
aluminum rather than a wood top to amplify its sound.
With a distinctly bright tone, so-called resonator
guitars were offered with a set-up that allowed for
regular-style playing or one in which the strings were
set high above the fingerboard and fretted with a
steel bar held in the left hand. The instrument
illustrated here has a square neck made for the latter
"Hawaiian style" of playing and is held flat on the
player's lap. But the loud and twangy sound of
resonator guitars also appealed greatly to blues and
country musicians, most of whom played examples
with a neck whose back side was rounded like that on
a regular guitar.

First manufactured in 1927, the Tri-cone is the earliest
of various designs for a resonator guitar created by
the performer George Beauchamp and John Dopyera. As
the name implies, the Tri-cone employs three shallow
aluminum cones (covered by grillwork in the lower half
of the body) to amplify the sound of the strings, which
are acoustically coupled to the cones by a T-shaped
bridge. The Tri-cone also has a hollow neck for added
resonance, a feature Dopyera may have adopted from the
wooden Hawaiian-style guitars made by a neighboring
craftsman named Hermann Weissenborn. At least as
radical as the Tri-cone's acoustical structures are its
body and neck of nickel alloy covered with shiny nickel-
silver plating. The gleaming metallic finish and geometric latticework are distinctly in the Art Deco style, but
this "Machine Age" look is oddly juxtaposed with delicate engraved flowers on the front, back, and sides that
are much more Victorian in flavor.

Nickel silver, ebony, plastic
L. 98 cm, w. 36.2 cm, d. 8.4 cm (L. 38 9/16 in., w. 14 1/4 in., d. 3 5/16 in.)
Helen B. Sweeney Fund 1998.193

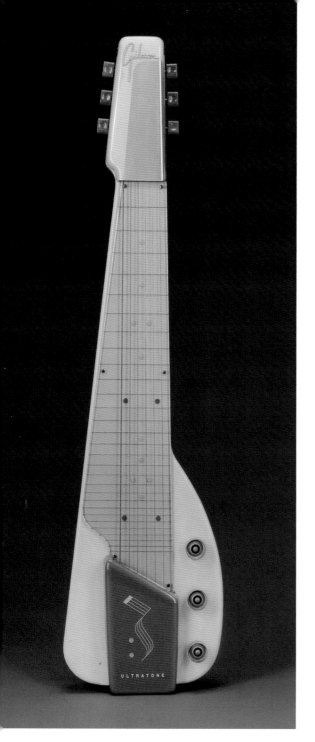

Lap steel guitar (Ultratone model)

Gibson, Inc.

United States (Kalamazoo, Michigan)

About 1949

Made in huge numbers between the 1930s and 1950s, "lap steels" were the first commercially successful electric guitars. Their popularity was directly linked to the craze for Hawaiian music, for which their playing style, using a bar in the left hand to create a sliding, glissando effect on the strings, was aptly suited. Apart from those who play its technologically advanced descendant, the pedal steel, few perform on lap steels today.

After World War II, Gibson and many other guitar manufacturers were sure that interest in Hawaiian music and lap steels would continue with the same vigor it had experienced during the 1930s. So in 1946, Gibson confidently launched its high-styled Ultratone model, featuring it on the cover of its first post-war catalogue in 1949. Gibson enlisted the aid of the indus-trial design firm Barnes and Reinecke in Chicago to create the sleek, streamlined body of the Ultratone, whose styling is not unlike household appliances of the time. Although the body is of wood, its rounded corners imitate the look of molded plastic, while the soft ivory finish is comple-mented by bright coral tuning knobs and pickup cover to create an especially harmo-nious color scheme. During its years of production, the Ultratone was offered in various decorator colors, including salmon and deep blue.

Sadly for Gibson, the post-war period saw a declining interest in the carefree sound of Hawaiian music, as more vigorous genres like jazz and eventually rock and roll took its place. No amount of good looks could save the Ultratone and other lap steels from losing out to regular electric guitars, which were quickly becoming perfected and were certainly more versatile – and in which the resourceful Gibson also became a leader.

Maple, plastic

L. 83 cm, w. 20.5 cm, d. 4.7 cm

(L. 32 11/16 in., w. 8 1/16 in., d. 1 7/8 in.)

Museum purchase with funds donated by Gibson Guitar Corp.

2001.239

Fiddle (*sindhī sāraṅgī*)

India (possibly Kotah, Rajasthan)

19th century

Originating in the region of present-day Pakistan, the
sāraṅgī is a variant of short-necked fiddle distributed
throughout southern Asia. There are many different
forms and sizes of *sāraṅgī*, from large, elaborate instruments used for classical music to smaller, simpler types
used in folk genres. Ornamentation ranges from extrav-
agant to relatively restrained; the painted decoration
on this particular folk *sāraṅgī* is in the tradition of north
Indian miniature painting. The body and neck of such
fiddles are typically constructed from one piece of
hollowed-out wood, the waisted belly covered with a thin
piece of goatskin. Thick sheep gut is used for the three
main playing strings, but as with many chordophones
of the Indian subcontinent, the *sāraṅgī* also has several
sympathetic strings of metal. Played by a master performer, a concert-size *sāraṅgī* produces a remarkably
resonant and soulful tone.

    The *sāraṅgī* is held in the performer's lap and played
with a bowing method that is jerky and emphatic, providing a kind of rhythmic accompaniment for a solo singer.
Another noteworthy aspect of its playing technique
is that the cuticles of the left-hand fingers (often pro-
tected by tape) press the playing strings from the side to
change the pitch, rather than pressing them down as
with Western string instruments. *Sāraṅgī* players were
required to be competent in a wide range of musical
genres, including song and dance, and as such were once
among the region's most highly esteemed musicians.
During India's British period, however, they became
somewhat stigmatized through their association with
courtesan singers and dances. Although the situation
gradually improved, the *sāraṅgī* is seldom heard in modern-day concerts.

Wood, goatskin

L. 54.8 cm, w. 14.8 cm, d. 9.8 cm

(L. 21 ⅝ in., w. 5 ¹³⁄₁₆ in., d. 3 ¹³⁄₁₆ in.)

Samuel Putnam Avery Fund   1985.725

Fiddle (*sǫ ū*)

Thailand

About 1975

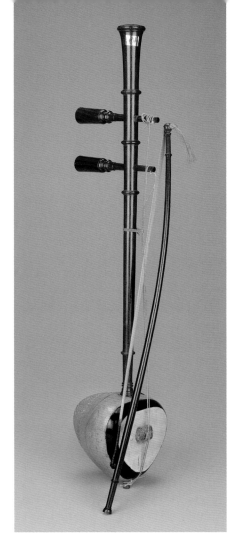

Throughout Asia, the majority of traditional bowed string instruments are of a form called a spike fiddle. In this type of instrument, a long, slender neck pierces a relatively small body from top to bottom, protruding at the lower end and providing a spike or knob to which the strings are tied. The bodies of these fiddles are made from a wide range of materials, including wood, bamboo, coconut, and even ivory. Covering the front surface of the hollow body is a thin material that serves as a soundtable, occasionally wood, but more often the skin of a mammal or reptile. Spike fiddles do not have a separate fingerboard against which the strings are pressed. Instead, the strings are lightly touched or "stopped" with fingers of the left hand to select the required notes.

The generic name for fiddles in Thailand is *sǫ* (pronounced saw), and there are three distinct types used for various kinds of music, the *sǫ sām sāi*, *sǫ duang*, and *sǫ ū*. The *sǫ sām sāi* has three strings, while the latter two instruments are each set up with only a pair. Both the *sǫ sām sāi* and *sǫ ū* have bodies constructed from half of a coconut shell, with soundtables made of goatskin or calfskin. The body of the *sǫ duang* is tubular, though, made from wood or bamboo and usually covered with snakeskin, often that of a python or boa constrictor. Like the *erhu* and other Chinese spike fiddles, the bow hair of the *sǫ ū* passes between the instrument's two silk strings. In playing, the bow is pulled against the lower string and pushed against the upper one, which are tuned to the musical interval of a fifth. The *sǫ ū* is pitched lower than the *sǫ duang*, its higher string tuned to the same note as the lower string of the *sǫ duang*. In ensemble performance, the two instruments may duplicate the melody in octaves or play in a style of statement and response. With both types of instrument, the performer is seated on the floor with the fiddle's body resting on the left thigh. The *sǫ ū* illus-trated here shows typical features of such an instrument, the coconut body pierced by a turned spike of tropical hardwood that flares slightly at its upper end. The bridge, placed near the center of the calfskin head, is made from tightly rolled cloth. Carved in openwork design on the back of the body is the likeness of Hanuman, the magical white monkey warrior found in *Ramakien*, the Thai version of the Indian epic *Ramayana*.

Coconut, wood, calfskin
L. 63.9 cm, w. 12.8 cm, d. 12.4 cm
(L. 25 ⅜ in., w. 5 ⅛ in., d. 4 ⅞ in.)
Gift of Visuttichittra Vanichsombat   1978.1204a–b

Fiddle (*masenqo*)

Ethiopia

19th century

The African continent has relatively few indigenous bowed string instruments, and these are mostly limited to the regions in the west and northeast. Unlike the gourd fiddles of West Africa, which are held horizontally against the chest, Ethiopia's only bowed instrument is positioned vertically and is much more closely related to examples found in the Middle East, like the *rebab*. The body of the *masenqo* is sometimes square, but more commonly diamond-shaped, as in this example. The front and back of the wood body are open, each covered by tanned goatskins that are stitched together along the sides of the framework. Like other spike fiddles of Asia, this instrument's neck is inserted into a hole at the top of the body and protrudes out the bottom end. The *masenqo* has only one thick string (missing on the present instrument, as is the bridge) fashioned from several strands of horsehair. Its very short and highly curved bow is likewise fitted with horsehair.

Performers play the *masenqo* seated with the instrument between their knees and the neck resting against their left shoulder. Notes are stopped on the string using all the fingers and thumb of the left hand. Despite this fiddle's crude structure, players are capable of playing with considerable virtuosity, using harmonics and vibrato. The tone is considered muted, yet strident. Made only in one size, the *masenqo* is used almost entirely for secular music, especially by troubadours accompanying songs. Improvised solo preludes and interludes may also be interspersed between song verses. Most highland villages of Ethiopia have at least one *masenqo* player, and as many as twenty *masenqo*s may be played together at certain festivals.

Olive wood, goatskin

L. 89.6 cm, w. 33.2 cm, d. 10.5 cm

(L. 35 ¼ in., w. 13 ⅛ in., d. 4 ⅛ in.)

Leslie Lindsey Mason Collection   17.2190a–b

Fiddle (*kízh kízh díhí*)
White Mountain Apache people
United States (Arizona)
19th century

Curious little tubular fiddles such as this are the only string instrument made by the native peoples of North America, although it is unknown how far back their use extends and whether they might, in fact, have been influenced by observation of the string instruments of early Spanish settlers. They are found only in the Southwest region among the Apache people and in sections of Southern California. In the Apache language, the instrument's onomatopoeic name *kízh kízh díhí* means "buzz buzz sound," which relates to the soft, squeaky tone produced by its single string made from strands of horsehair. An alternative name is *tsii' edo' áłi*, which means "wood singing."

Constructed from the stalk of an agave or mescal plant, the body may be hollowed out after first splitting the stalk lengthwise, or the pith may be removed through a large soundhole cut in the side. A modest instrument by any measure, this type of fiddle is always played by itself, and usually only for personal pleasure. This particular example is covered with detailed painted decoration consisting of geometric figures meant to represent various objects from nature. Not all of these symbols have been deciphered, but the bow-tie shapes probably represent butterflies, the semicircles may be clouds, and the black diagonal lines perhaps indicate rain.

Agave stalk
L. 31.5 cm, diam. 4.3 cm (L. 12⅜ in., diam. 1¹¹⁄₁₆ in.)
Leslie Lindsey Mason Collection   17.2239a–b

Violin

Nicolo Amati, 1596–1684

Italy (Cremona)

1641 (with later alterations)

Few musical instrument have commanded as much attention, respect, and mystique over the centuries as the violin. Players enthuse about the tone of great instruments, historians and dealers study the subtle details of each master luthier's work, and collectors pay top dollar for the rarest and most sought-after examples. Instruments made in northern Italy have long been particularly esteemed by violin lovers, and it was here that a well-developed form for the instrument was established by 1550, one that has changed very little since. Much of the credit for the violin's early presence in Italy is given to Gasparo da Salo in Brescia and Andrea Amati in Cremona. Both towns remained centers of excellent violin making into the eighteenth century, although Cremona hosted a greater number of luminaries, including the families Guarneri and Bergonzi and succeeding generations of the Amati clan. Cremona was also the workplace of Antonio Stradivari, the only instrument maker who truly has name recognition throughout the world.

Nicolo Amati, grandson of Andrea, was also an extremely talented luthier, and it is believed that he was a teacher of Stradivari. A plague nearly wiped out Cremona's violin-making population during the seventeenth century, but Nicolo was fortunately not among the fatalities, leaving him as the only master maker to carry on the craft and pass along its secrets to the next generation. Virtually all of the old Cremonese instruments were modernized during the nineteenth century, acquiring a longer neck and fingerboard, and a stronger internal strut (called a bass bar) to make them capable of withstanding greater string tension and playing higher notes. In addition to these typical alterations, the belly of this Amati violin was at some time replaced with one made by Carlo Tononi of Bologna, another respected early luthier. It nonetheless remains a very fine instrument, with a sound that is spontaneous, noble, and intimate.

The seemingly simple form of a violin belies the fact that over seventy separate pieces of wood are required to create one instrument. Violin makers still employ the finest spruce and maple, striving to emulate the tone and beauty of instruments created by celebrated luthiers of the past. They have yet to discover the exact formulation of varnish used by the old masters, but the notion that excellent violin tone is related to an instrument's finish was long ago debunked. Some musicians bemoan the presence of fine violins in museum collections, but the vast majority of these instruments are, in fact, still in circulation among professional performers.

Maple, spruce, ebony
L. 58.5 cm, w. 20.1 cm, d. 3.1 cm
(L. 23 1/16 in., w. 7 15/16 in., d. 1 1/4 in.)
Gift of Arthur E. Spiller, M.D. 1991.73

Dance master's violin

Georg Wörle, about 1620–1675
Germany (Augsburg)
1673

Given how highly esteemed the violin is as a musical instrument today, it is interesting to note that during its early history it had rather low social standing. The problem was that its sprightly sound was considered more suited to the accompaniment of dancing than to the performance of serious music. That association has, in a sense, lingered with the violin even into modern times, as we think of fiddlers providing the tune for a traditional Scottish reel or an American barn dance.

This diminutive violin is a type of instrument that was played from the sixteenth through the nineteenth centuries by dance instructors. Although the sound was delicate, it was loud enough to provide music for private dance lessons that took place in a small chamber. The petite size permitted the instrument to be carried in a gentleman's coat pocket, hence its French names *poche* or *pochette* (referring to pocket). In England it was usually called a kit, which may be short for kitten, i.e., something smaller than full size.

Dance masters' violins were constructed in two basic forms, one with a narrow boat-shaped body, the other with a tiny violin-shaped body. Perhaps because of their simple outline, the boat-shaped instruments were often more highly decorated with various precious materials. The faceted back of this instrument is beautifully veneered with tortoiseshell, accented by thin ivory strips. Atop the pegbox is a finely carved head of an exotic African woman, wearing a dainty beaded necklace and earrings.

Spruce, tortoiseshell, ebony, ivory
L. 26 cm, w. 3.5 cm, d. 2.8 cm (L. 10¼ in., w. 1⅜ in., d. 1⅛ in.)
Gift of Mr. and Mrs. Richard M. Fraser,
and Arthur Tracy Cabot Fund 1995.123

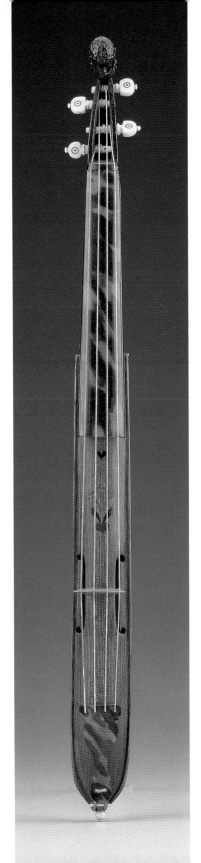

Bass viola da gamba
Attributed to Claude Pierray, working 1698–1729
France (Paris)
About 1710

The viola da gamba is from a distinctly different family of bowed string instruments from the violin; and all of its members, from treble to bass, are held upright between the players' legs (the term *gamba*, in fact, means "leg" in Italian). Other differences from the violin family include six strings tuned in fourths rather than four strings tuned in fifths, a flat-backed body with sloping shoulders, C-shaped soundholes, and gut frets tied around the fingerboard. Frets are present because the viol, as it is often simply called, developed from an instrument called the *vihuela*, which was rather like a guitar and could be alternatively played by plucking the strings with the fingers or stroking them with a bow.

By the late 1500s, a consort of viols was considered the most noble instrumental ensemble one could employ for the performance of "serious" contrapuntal music. But the playing of viols began to decline during the eighteenth century as the violin grew in prominence. The bass size was the last type of viola da gamba to retain significant popularity, especially in France. There, a low seventh string was added to enhance the instrument's ability to perform a substantial solo repertoire, developed by French players such as Marin Marais and Antoine Forqueray. This unsigned instrument attributed to Claude Pierray is one of only a handful of such seven-string instruments from the French school to survive into modern times.

Maple, spruce
L. 129 cm, w. 40 cm, d. 14 cm
(L. 50 13/16 in., w. 15 3/4 in., d. 5 1/2 in.)
Leslie Lindsey Mason Collection   17.1717

Viola d'amore
Southern Germany
About 1710

The viola d'amore is a curious instrument whose history is still not fully understood. Its body shape shares features with the viola da gamba, such as sloping shoulders and a flat back. Likewise, the edges of the back and belly are cut flush with the sides of the body, rather than slightly overhanging as in a violin. But the instrument is held like a violin and has no frets on its fingerboard. Although firm evidence is lacking, some historians have suggested that the viola d'amore descended from a bowed instrument of the Arabic world, and that its name is a corruption of "viol of the Moor." Soundholes in the shape of flames, an Islamic symbol, are thought to reinforce this theory.

Besides five main strings lying on its fingerboard, this viola d'amore has a group of seven metal strings running beneath the fingerboard that are not bowed by the player, but that vibrate sympathetically with the main strings. One does not actually hear the sympathetic strings as separate notes, but they contribute to the overall timbre to create a clear, resonant tone that has been described as soft and silvery. This "lovely" sound is probably the most likely source for the name viola d'amore. The theme of love is highlighted on many surviving instruments, including this one, by a blindfolded cupid carved atop the pegbox.

Whatever its true origins, the viola d'amore was popular only from the late seventeenth century to the end of the eighteenth century. Most of the known instruments were constructed in southern Germany and surrounding areas, although it was included in works by composers active in various parts of Europe, such as Telemann, Vivaldi, and Bach. The few solo works written for the viola d'amore often make use of alternate tunings for the strings, called *scordatura*.

Maple, spruce, ebony
L. 75 cm, w. 24.2 cm, d. 3.8 cm
(L. 29½ in., w. 9½ in., d. 1½ in.)
Leslie Lindsey Mason Collection 17.1719

Hardanger violin (*hardingfela*)
Jørgen Knudsen, working 1830s
Norway (Hardanger region)
1838

A distinctive type of violin was developed in western Norway, apparently during the middle of the eighteenth century, that ultimately became the country's national instrument. These violins remain popular in Norway today, where performance competitions help maintain knowledge and interest in their traditional repertoire. Characteristics of the older examples (predating 1860) include a narrow, angular body, highly arched belly and back, elongated soundholes, and a relative abundance of ornamentation. The earliest Hardanger violins also exhibit construction techniques that appear to be retained from archaic methods used by regular violin makers who were once active in other parts of northern Europe. By the late nineteenth century, the body of the *hardingfela* became more violinlike in form and fabrication, but retained its traditional decoration, derived from regional motifs.

A singular musical feature of the Hardanger violin is the presence of four wire strings running beneath the fingerboard, which resonate when notes are played on the main strings. It has not been determined with any certainty whether these were adopted in emulation of the viola d'amore, but this seems a likely hypothesis. Because the instrument's traditional repertoire of folksongs and dances does not require moving one's fingers very far up the neck, the neck and the fingerboard are relatively short compared to those of a regular violin. Likewise, the fingerboard and bridge are comparatively flat, since much of the instrument's music makes use of double stops, in which two strings are bowed simultaneously.

The pegbox of many Hardanger violins terminates in a carved head of a lion or dragon, although this early example by Jørgen Knudsen has, instead, a somewhat undersized scroll like that on a regular violin. The bodies of such instruments are also often profusely decorated with borders of flowers, leaves, and geometric designs, executed in India ink. The Knudsen instrument's ornamentation is quite restrained, however, consisting primarily of a checkerboard pattern of bone and wood overlay on the fingerboard.

Maple, pine
L. 56 cm, w. 18.8 cm, d. 3.3 cm (L. 22 ¹/₁₆ in., w. 7 ³/₈ in., d. 1 ⁵/₁₆ in.)
Leslie Lindsey Mason Collection   17.1722a–b

Cither viol (*sultana*)
Perry and Wilkinson
Ireland (Dublin)
1794

A rare and unusual instrument, the cither viol (also inexplicably called the *sultana*) differs from other bowed string instruments of the eighteenth century in having several pairs of metal strings rather than individual ones of gut. Its exact musical uses are unclear, but the cither viol appears to have been intended as a bowed companion to the popular "English guitar," a type of cittern of the period similarly tuned. Of the few examples of this instrument preserved in museums today, this one is perhaps the most elegant, with an ivory-veneered fingerboard and tailpiece and gold-plated, geared tuners for the strings.

Maple, spruce, ivory, brass
L. 71.2 cm, w. 23 cm, d. 3.7 cm
(L. 28 ¹/₁₆ in., w. 9 ¹/₁₆ in., d. 1 ⁷/₁₆ in.)
Leslie Lindsey Mason Collection   17.1725

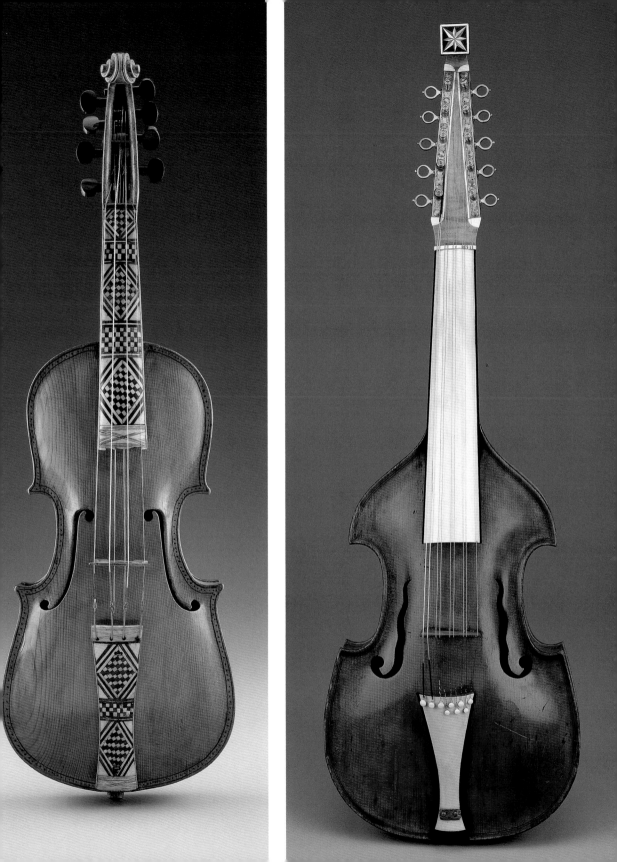

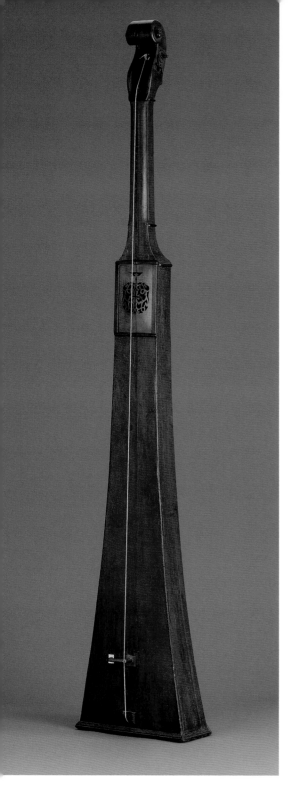

Trumpet marine

France

About 1700

The trumpet marine is not a bass instrument, despite its great length. It is designed to play high harmonic notes produced by lightly touching its single string at various points while bowing close to the upper end of the neck. The sound is surprisingly similar to that of a muted trumpet, which is caused by an asymmetrical bridge, one leg of which is designed to vibrate rapidly against the instrument's belly, creating a buzzing quality to the tone. The exact reason for use of the term "marine" in this instrument's name remains obscure, despite considerable research by scholars. A small version of the trumpet marine was in use during the fifteenth and sixteenth centuries, but the instrument's heyday, in the larger form pictured here, was from about 1650 to 1725.

Despite certain of its notes being considerably out of tune (a natural phenomenon of the so-called harmonic series), over 300 works of music were composed for the trumpet marine in both ensemble and solo settings, including pieces by such well-known composers as Jean-Baptiste Lully and Allesandro Scarlatti. A curious aspect of the instrument's history is that in German-speaking countries it was often played in convents by nuns; hence one of its alternate names, *Nonnengeige*, or nun's fiddle. Although for several decades modern musicians have been reviving instruments from earlier times, the trumpet marine is almost never heard today, either in live performance or on recordings.

Pine
L. 192 cm, w. 36.5 cm, d. 24.5 cm
(L. 75⁹⁄₁₆ in., w. 14³⁄₈ in., d. 9⁵⁄₈ in.)
Leslie Lindsey Mason Collection   17.1733

Double bass

Abraham Prescott, 1789–1858
United States (Deerfield, New Hampshire)
1823

With few immigrants trained in the art of lutherie and a relatively low product demand, it is not surprising that violins and related instruments were seldom made in the United States before the 1790s. Much of puritan New England maintained a lingering sentiment against instrumental music in general, and many considered the violin's long association with dancing especially damning. But in the early decades of the nineteenth century, many of the region's rural churches that could not afford a pipe organ began to use cellos and basses to provide instrumental support for congregational singing. With their deep, somber tone, they were considered more acceptable instruments for worship than the sprightly violin. The basic playing technique for a cello or bass could also be learned by a member of a congregation in a fairly short time, without formal study. As demand for these low-pitched instruments increased, several self-taught makers began to manufacture them locally, further motivated by the difficulty and expense of importing such large and fragile instruments from abroad.

During this time, Southern New Hampshire was New England's most active region for the production of all sorts of musical instruments, including cellos and basses. Abraham Prescott was the area's most noted string instrument builder, working first in Deerfield, then setting up a manufactory in nearby Concord in 1831, which at times employed as many as six men building hundreds of instruments through the mid-1840s. Prescott and his contemporaries usually advertised their cello-type instruments as "bass viols" or "single bass viols," while the term double bass denoted the larger instruments. Numerous examples of Prescott's single basses survive, and although they are generally well-built instruments, they are difficult to adapt to modern playing because their bodies are considerably longer and wider than that of standard size cellos. But Prescott's double basses, made in various sizes and shapes, are highly prized by players of both classical music and jazz. They have almost invariably been modernized, however, to the now-standard arrangement of four strings, rather than preserved in the original three-string setup seen on this example.

Maple, pine
L. 190 cm, w. 68.2 cm, d. 18 cm
(L. 74 13/16 in., w. 26 7/8 in.,
d. 7 1/8 in.)
Gift of Frank G. Webster
1987.22

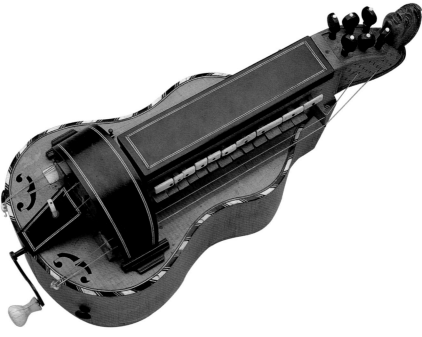

Hurdy-gurdy
Joseph Bassot, 1750–1808
France (Mirecourt)
About 1775

The hurdy-gurdy has existed since the Middle Ages and was often depicted in the hands of beggars and itinerant musicians. In its modern form, the strings (some of which sound only a drone) are vibrated by a wooden wheel coated with rosin and turned with a metal crank by the right hand. The fingers of the left hand are used to push sliding wood keys (housed in a rectangular box atop the body) with tabs mounted on them that press against the two melody strings and change their pitch. A small amount of cotton is wrapped around the strings where they contact the wheel, allowing them to speak somewhat better. The tone is quite raspy and the constant drone, like that heard on a bagpipe, can become tiresome, but both features are functions of the instrument's rustic musical character.

The French aristocracy took up the hurdy-gurdy in the second half of the seventeenth century, using it as a functional prop in their affected role-playing of pastoral life. By the 1720s, however, more sophisticated music began to be composed for the instrument, including works by Boismortier, Corrette, and Rameau. Also during this time, two basic forms were developed for the body of the hurdy-gurdy, one shaped like a guitar (as illustrated here), and another with a curved back like a lute. By the onset of the nineteenth century, the hurdy-gurdy had become an instrument used only for regional folk music, mostly in central France, but today interest in the instrument has been somewhat revived and is more widespread.

Maple, spruce, ebony, ivory
L. 71 cm, w. 26.5 cm, d. 10.5 cm
(L. 27 15/16 in., w. 10 7/16 in., d. 4 1/8 in.)
Leslie Lindsey Mason Collection 17.1735

Keyed fiddle (*nyckelharpa*)

Sweden

Early 19th century

Dating back to at least the middle of the fourteenth century, the *nyckelharpa*'s history is documented in Germany, Denmark, and various other parts of Scandinavia. As its popularity for dance and festive music waned, though, it was only in the Swedish province of Uppland that a living tradition of playing the instrument was maintained into the twentieth century. Revival of the *nyckelharpa* in the 1970s, prompted by an increased interest in folk music generally, is a true success story, as only a handful of the instrument's aged practitioners were still living at the time, virtually none of whom performed publicly. It is one of the few European musical instruments currently in use that is essentially unchanged since the Middle Ages. Modern researchers and players have now thoroughly explored the roots of the *nyckelharpa*, recovering traditional tunes but also creating new ones in the same spirit.

The *nyckelharpa* has been constructed in slightly different forms throughout the centuries, but an elongated body with small in-curved bouts, like that seen here, is fairly common. The number and arrangement of strings has also varied greatly, even in recent times. On this example, the melody is produced from two main strings by raising the wood keys along the neck with the left hand. This mechanism for selecting notes is the same as that used in the hurdy-gurdy, and it has yet to be discovered how the two instruments might have influenced each other in their early histories. Of the various other strings, some provide a growling drone while others are sympathetic strings that resonate to vibrations from the melody strings. The bow, held in the right hand, is short and outwardly curved. A woven cloth strap helps hold the *nyckelharpa* to the performer's body and allows it to be played in either a sitting or standing position.

Pine

L. 83 cm, w. 18.5 cm, d. 9.5 cm

(L. 32 11/16 in., w. 7 5/16 in., d. 3 3/4 in.)

Leslie Lindsey Mason Collection   17.1734a–b

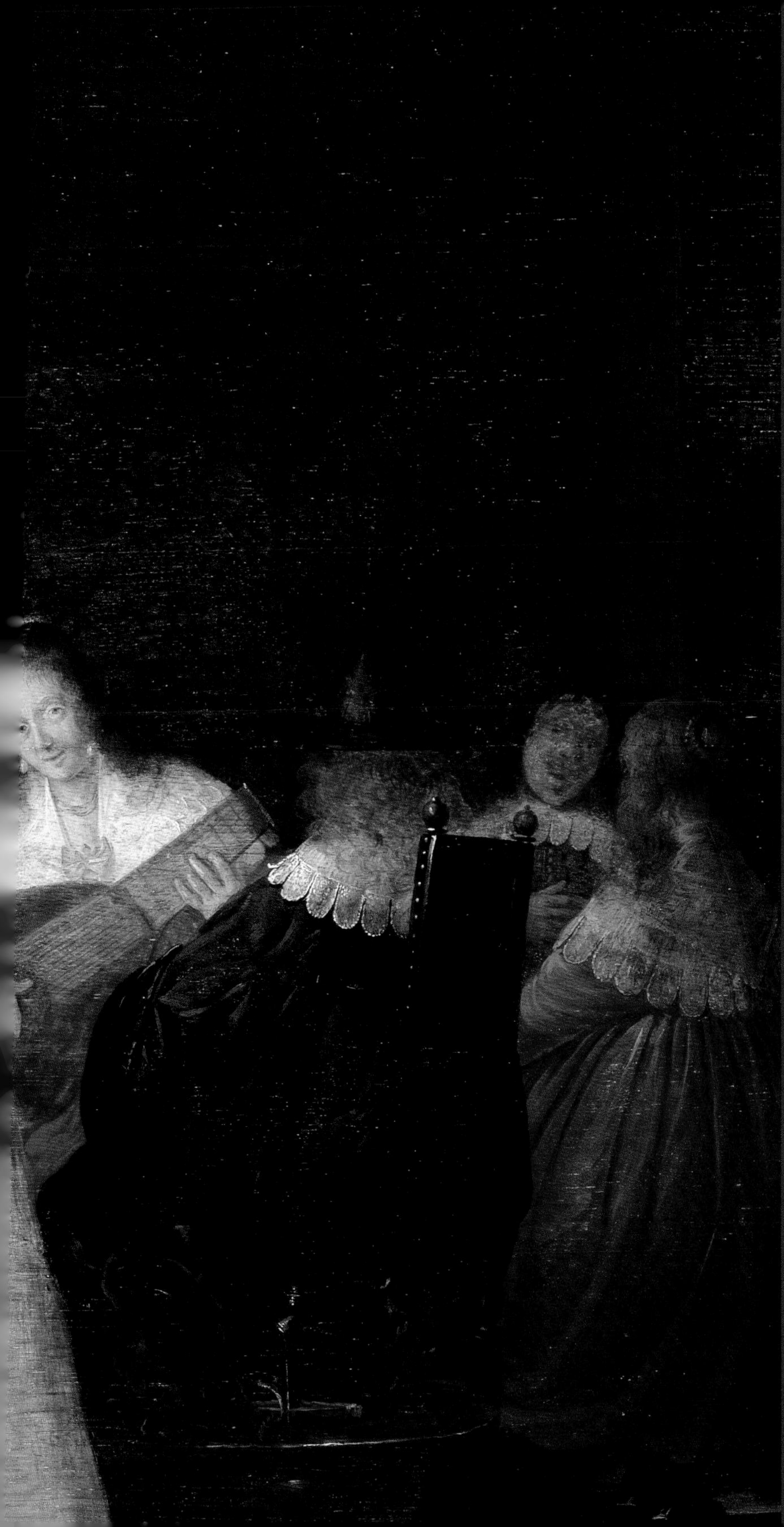

4 KEYBOARD instruments

Keyboard Instruments

Keyboard instruments are the most complex musical instruments mechanically, and as such it is useful to group them together in their own separate chapter. This diverges somewhat from the categorizations in other sections of the book, for different keyboard instruments may fall into each of these categories. The harpsichord, clavichord, and piano all have strings, activated by varying mechanisms. The organ, conversely, is a wind instrument, which may be constructed with pipes or reeds activated by pressurized air.

The sophistication and size of keyboard instruments means that they are relatively expensive. Consequently, ownership of a piano or organ was, and often still is, indicative of its buyer's wealth and status. When used in the home, they are often displayed in a prominent position, where they also assume a role as furniture. With legs to support them and large, flat surfaces constituting their casework, keyboard instruments lend themselves to ornamentation, and one can find an endless variety of decorative treatments employed over the centuries, including elaborate painting, intricate marquetry, exotic veneers, and detailed carving.

The great popularity of keyboard instruments stems from their ability to provide a complete musical experience, with melody, harmony, and considerable volume. Most keyboard instruments have a significant body of solo repertoire, much of it created by some of the most outstanding composers of the past four hundred years. But they are also ideal as accompaniment to other instruments and to the human voice. With only a modicum of talent one can even sing while playing, a pastime that used to occupy many an evening before the advent of radio and television. Both the piano and organ have been nominated for the title "King of Instruments" by their partisans, and we won't attempt to resolve the debate here. Suffice it to say that all keyboard instruments have a rich and musically varied history that is still being rediscovered and added to by generations of players.

fig. 27 (preceding page) **Godaert Kamper**, German (active in Holland), 1613 or 1614–1679, *Musical Party*, oil on panel, Gift of Mrs. Albert J. Beveridge in memory of Delia Spencer Field, 46.842

fig. 28 (above) **Hans Burgkmair the Elder**, German, 1473–1531, *Triumphal Procession of Maximilian*, woodcut, Gift of Robert Treat Paine, Jr., M35721.22 (depicted is the composer Paul Hofhaimer playing an organ)

Organ (regal)

Marked: Simon Bauer and *C. E.*
Austria or southern Germany
1692

The principal form of pipe used in organs is the very ancient type with a flue, functioning like the wood-wind instrument called a recorder, with a duct that directs air past a sharp whistlelike edge. Of much more recent vintage – dating only to the early fifteenth century – is another form called a reed pipe. In this style of pipe, sound is produced when a thin brass tongue vibrates or beats against the open top surface of a semicylindrical structure of metal or wood, similar in appearance and function to a clarinet mouthpiece with its affixed reed. The "mouthpiece" section, called a shallot, is coupled to a resonator of varying size, which amplifies and modifies the raw sound of the reed. The term regal can be used to denote either a set of short reed pipes, included among several other ranks of pipes in a large organ, or a small, portable organ that only contains such reed pipes. It is unknown in which of these circumstances reed pipes were first used, and the etymology of the word regal is likewise uncertain.

Regals like the one shown here are very rare, and this instrument bears the name Simon Bauer inscribed on one of its reeds, while an interior wood surface of the case bears a handwritten date of 1692

and the initials C. E. Nothing whatsoever is known of the identity of either of these craftspeople, but the presence of German text on the recycled papers that line the inside of the bellows strongly suggests the instrument's regional origins. This regal is of a type that is especially portable: the keyboard can be removed, then stored and transported inside the pair of bellows, which are hinged to fold against one another. When the instrument is played, an assistant is required to pump the bellows for the performer.

The regal was used for both solo and ensemble playing during the Renaissance and Baroque eras. Its beating reeds produce a strong buzzing tone that is especially effective in combination with other instruments, where it can compete on a more equal footing than the harpsichord, in terms of both volume and its ability to sustain. One of the most noted uses of the regal is in Claudio Monteverdi's 1607 opera *Orfeo*, where, for dramatic effect, he calls for its snarling tone to accompany a scene set in the underworld.

Walnut case
L. 101.5 cm, w. 65.7 cm, h. 9.9 cm
(L. 39 ¹⁵⁄₁₆ in., w. 25 ⅞ in., h. 3 ⅞ in.) The Edward F. Searles Musical Instrument Collection; given by Edward S. Rowland, Benjamin A. Rowland, Jr., George B. Rowland, Daniel B. Rowland, Rodney D. Rowland, and M. A. Swedlund in Memory of their father, Benjamin Allen Rowland   1981.746

fig. 29 (opposite) **Detail of virginal by Joseph Salodiensis (see p. 153)**

Lap organ (melodeon)

Prescott and Son
United States (Concord, New Hampshire)
About 1845

A peripatetic Yankee inventor named James A. Bazin, working in Canton, Massachusetts, devised the first lap organ in 1836. Soon thereafter a more business-savvy instrument maker in Concord, New Hampshire, Abraham Prescott, purchased one of Bazin's lap organs from a Boston merchant and began manufacturing similar instruments on a commercial scale. Bazin expressed his resentment of Prescott's product thievery in an article published in 1853 in *The Musical World and Times*, but he was probably naive to have not patented his design in the first place. Examples of Prescott's lap organs are now relatively plentiful, whereas Bazin's instruments are exceedingly rare.

Modest instruments like this were the first reed organs manufactured in the United States, where their portability and relatively low cost made them popular for use in rural churches, especially in New England. The lap organ is somewhat complicated to operate, however, as the performer must continuously depress the left end of the case with the left forearm to pump air to the reeds, while simultaneously manipulating the ivory button-type keys with both hands – hence one of the instrument's vernacular names, elbow melodeon. The to-and-fro motion of the top gave rise to other epithets as well, including rocking melodeon and teeter. Although the instrument may, in fact, be placed on the player's lap, better control is offered by resting it on a table or two chairs, as shown in a few period depictions of the instrument.

Rosewood and maple case
L. 57.6 cm, w. 29.2 cm, h. 12.4 cm
(L 22 ⁷⁄₁₆ in., w. 11 ½ in., h. 4 ⁷⁄₈ in.)
Samuel Putnam Avery Fund   2002.380

fig. 30 (above) **Alfred Little of Concord, New Hampshire, playing a lap organ, from** *The History of Boscawen and Webster from 1733 to 1878* **(Concord, NH: The Republican Press Association, 1878).**

Polygonal virginal

Joseph Salodiensis, dates unknown
Italy
1574

One of the Museum's oldest European instruments, this virginal is an exquisite example of the small keyboards used in domestic settings, where they were sometimes positioned against a wall. Like a harpsichord, a virginal employs a mechanism that plucks its thin metal strings, producing an incisive tone. The earliest virginals of the fifteenth century, which no longer survive, were most likely built with rectangular cases, but by the sixteenth century Italian makers were producing a polygonal shape like the one shown here, which is a lighter and more graceful form.

In this particular instrument, the virginal itself, constructed from thin panels of cypress, can be completely removed from its protective outer case, which is made of painted spruce. This inner/outer style of construction is common in Italian virginals and harpsichords. The outer case of this virginal is original to the instrument, but most of its painted decoration, regrettably, is not, although some of the gold Moresque borders on the lid and arabesques ornamenting an interior storage compartment do, in fact, appear to date from the late sixteenth or early seventeenth century. Virtually all music from this period only goes as high as the note C that lies two octaves above middle C. This Italian virginal, however, like most others of the time, has five additional notes in the treble, extending up to F. The reason, interestingly enough, may have been to simply create a keyboard with a width that was in better proportion to the case itself, and likewise more centered in its position.

Cypress case
L. 158.6 cm, w. 48.1 cm, h. 17.9 cm
(L. 62 7/16 in., w. 19 5/16 in., h. 7 1/16 in.)
Frank B. Bemis Fund   1981.277

Clavichord

Italy

Late 16th or early 17th century

With few exceptions, clavichords are built with rectangular cases, their thin brass strings running longitudinally. The strings are sounded when they are gently struck by small metal tabs, called tangents, one of which stands upright at the far end of each key. Because the tangent also determines one end of the string's stopped or sounding length – in a manner similar to a finger pressing down on a violin string against its fingerboard – the resulting energy to the string is very limited and the tone, therefore, very quiet. Even so, the clavichord is extremely responsive to the touch of the player, who can produce fine dynamic gradations down to an imperceptibly soft pianissimo. Since the tangent remains touching the string as long as the key is depressed, the performer can vary the string's tension slightly by gently moving his or her finger up and down. This creates an expressive, vibrato effect that is unique among keyboard instruments.

Clavichords are too quiet to be played with other instruments, but they were used widely for intimate solo performances and as a practice instrument. It is not until the second half of the eighteenth century that one finds a repertoire specifically composed for the clavichord, and during that time several German composers, most notably Carl Philipp Emanuel Bach, created a small but significant body of works. But much of the other solo keyboard music of the Baroque and Classical eras can also be successfully performed on the clavichord. The delicate tone of the instrument eventually succumbed to the louder and more versatile sound of the piano, but not before its range was expanded to five octaves of notes or more. The rare example illustrated here is one of only about eight surviving clavichords made before the middle of the seventeenth century, most of which are Italian.

Spruce case

L. 116.8 cm, w. 39.3 cm, h. 14.8 cm

(L. 46 in., w. 15½ in., h. 5¹³⁄₁₆ in.)

Leslie Lindsey Mason Collection   17.1796

Spinet
Stephen Keene, working 1655–about 1720
England (London)
1700

A spinet is a small type of harpsichord with a very compact, triangular case. With only one keyboard and one set of strings, spinets are relatively quiet and somewhat limited musically. But they were eminently suited to music making in the home, not only for the upper classes but also for merchants and other middle-class businessmen, who found this smallish instrument more affordable than a full-size harpsichord. It was primarily the daughters in a family who were enrolled for music lessons, striving to learn a few simple tunes with which they might entertain suitors who came to call. An ample supply of pleasant and easy music was published for the harpsichord during this period. In London, for example, Henry Purcell issued collections of pieces bearing titles such as "Musick's Hand-maid" and "The Ladys Banquet," which were apparently targeted toward female amateurs.

The use of ebony for a keyboard's natural notes and solid pieces of ivory for the accidentals was not unusual in 1700, but in the succeeding decades of the eighteenth century English keyboard-instrument makers began to swap those materials for the arrangement that we now consider normal. The keyboard of this Keene spinet has another interesting feature. The lowest two accidental notes are divided

Harpsichord

Henri Hemsch, (born Germany) 1700–1769
France (Paris)
Probably 1736

into front and back sections, and each half produces separate notes. This curious system allows for certain notes to be tuned in a manner called short-octave tuning, which extends the instrument's true range down to include a few notes that are occasionally called for in music of the period.

Although it is believed that the spinet was developed by an Italian maker named Girolamo Zenti, such instruments were especially popular in England. A few spinets were even built in the United States dur-

ing its Colonial period. As with most English keyboard instruments of the time, this spinet's case has a natural wood exterior rather than painted decoration. As an inexpensive instrument, it is also relatively plain, although the panel above the keys is nicely decorated with wood marquetry, incorporating a cat cozily nestled among pretty flowers and leaves. Stephen Keene was a prolific instrument maker, but apart from two early virginals, his entire surviving output is made up of spinets.

Walnut case
L. 162.4 cm, w. 60 cm, h. 17.3 cm
(L. 63¹⁵/₁₆ in., w. 23⅝ in., h. 6¹³/₁₆ in.)
Bequest of Charles Hitchcock Tyler   32.252

Several types of harpsichord were manufactured during the Baroque era, each with varying musical resources and decoration, depending on the country of origin. Eighteenth-century French harpsichords, however, are among the most sought-after by present-day performers and collectors, and are also the type most often copied by modern instrument makers. Their rich tonal palette is shown off to great effect in the works of French composers such as Couperin and Rameau, but they are also suitable for the music of foreign masters, such as Bach, Handel, and Scarlatti. This fine instrument by Henri Hemsch, with two keyboards and three registers of strings, provides all the musical resources considered desirable for performing this abundant and impressive repertoire.

The attractive flowers, birds, and insects painted on this harpsichord's soundboard are original, as is its carved and gilded stand, but the case exterior and lid were repainted in the early nineteenth century. The case's original decorative scheme may well have been much simpler. Armorial devices incorporated into the original decoration suggest that the instrument was at some point during the eighteenth century owned by Maximilien-Emmanuel-François-Joseph Wittelsbach and his wife, both members of a royal Bavarian family.

By 1800, the harpsichord's popularity was completely eclipsed by the piano, and a great many examples were lost or destroyed, particularly in France, where they were seized from the aristocracy in the wake of the French Revolution. Severe European winters of the early 1800s took a further toll, as many of these outmoded instruments were chopped up for firewood.

Henri Hemsch was born in Germany, as was his teacher, Antoine Vater, although both worked in Paris. Hemsch was very well regarded, with a clientele that included prominent musicians such as Claude Balbas-

tre and Louis-Claude Daqin. Five harpsichords from Hemsch's shop are known to survive, and the example shown is somewhat longer and of different design from the other four, which date between 1751 and 1762. Curiously, the third digit of its date of manufacture (painted on the soundboard) was at some time altered to make it read "1706," but given that Hemsch was born in 1700, this is quite implausible. Since the instrument is similar in design to the work of Vater, it was likely made by Hemsch during the earliest years that he worked independently, most probably in 1736. As a result of a full-scale technical drawing of this instrument that was published in 1976, the "Boston

Hemsch" has been replicated by numerous modern-day harpsichord builders throughout the world, though typically with much plainer decoration.

Painted poplar case
L. 238 cm, w. 89 cm, h. 28.3 cm
(L. 93 ¹¹/₁₆ in., w. 35 ⅛ in., h. 11⅛ in.)
The Edward F. Searles Musical Instrument Collection;
given by Edward S. Rowland, Benjamin A. Rowland, Jr.,
George B. Rowland, Daniel B. Rowland,
Rodney D. Rowland, and M. A. Swedlund in Memory of their
father, Benjamin Allen Rowland
1981.747

Grand piano
John Broadwood and Son
England (London)
1796

Considered the most richly decorated piano of its time, this instrument is also one of the most noteworthy objects of any type made in late-eighteenth-century England. It was commissioned by Manuel de Godoy, prime minister to King Carlos IV of Spain, from Broadwood and Son, the world's most prolific and, to many, most respected piano makers of the time. Celebrated English furniture designer Thomas Sheraton devised the decorative scheme for the casework, and this piano is the only known object designed by him for a specific commission, documented in a period engraving of his working drawing for the instrument. Nearly one hundred blue-and-white jasperware cameos created by the ceramicist Josiah Wedgwood adorn the satinwood and purpleheart veneer on the case exterior, while James Tassie's casts of ancient Greek coins frame the area above the keyboard. The legs, regrettably, are replace ments, probably dating from the early nineteenth century, as they do not match those shown in Sheraton's original drawing.

John Broadwood made his first grand pianos in 1781 or 1782, the appearance and internal framing of which are very similar to contemporary English harpsichords. Both types of instrument likewise possessed a five-octave range of notes from F to F. The pianos were outfitted with the recently developed "English grand action," a type that British manufacturers continued to use in their instruments through the end of the nineteenth century, with only slight improvements to the basic design. By the early 1790s, Broadwood began to introduce instruments with an extra half octave of notes at the treble end of the keyboard, extending up to the note C. Pianos with this five-and-a-half-octave range remained standard in Broadwood's output until about 1810, but by 1794 the

company had already produced a few grand pianos that also descended a half octave down to C at the bass end of the keyboard. Although the ornamentation of this Broadwood grand is truly impressive, the instrument is equally significant as the earliest surviving piano with a keyboard that possesses this range of six full octaves from C to C.

This remarkable instrument has been well known to piano historians for over a century, but there is a certain amount of confusion about its early ownership. It was clearly ordered by Godoy directly from Broadwood, and the company's surviving records bear witness to this fact. At an unknown date, however, an inscription was added to the Sheraton engraving of the piano (which resided in the Broadwood archives), indicating that this magnificent object was presented to Queen Maria Luisa as a gift from Godoy. If anything, though, it would have been more logical for the Queen to have given it to Godoy, since the two had none too secretly been lovers for years.

Satinwood, purpleheart, and tulipwood case
L. 248.7 cm, w. 111.5 cm, h. 28.4 cm
(L. 97 ¹⁵⁄₁₆ in., w. 43 ⅞ in., h. 11 ³⁄₁₆ in.)
From the George Alfred Cluett Collection,
Given by Florence Cluett Chambers
1985.924

Square piano

Benjamin Crehore, 1765–1831

United States (Milton, Massachusetts)

About 1800

The first commercially successful pianos were made and marketed by a German immigrant named Johannes Zumpe in London during the 1760s. This type of piano, with a rectangular case, remained by far the most prevalent in Europe and America through the 1830s. Broadwood and Sons, for example, produced about ten so-called square pianos for every one grand piano that came out of its shop. Square pianos were especially suited for use in the home, since they took up relatively little space and harmonized well with other furnishings. The sound of these instruments is softer and less sonorous than that of a grand piano (as is today's domestic upright piano), but it was more than ample for accompanying a singer or small group of other instruments in a modest-sized parlor or music room.

Benjamin Crehore was New England's first craftsman to leave behind a considerable number of signed musical instruments. At least sixteen pianos and cellos from his shop are known to survive, though it is said that he also produced violins, guitars, and drums. During his relatively short career as an instrument maker, he was in partnership with other Boston artisans, merchants, and musicians. One of Crehore's most lasting achievements was that he trained several Boston piano makers of the next generation, some of whom, notably Alpheus Babcock and John Osborne, were considerably more successful in this line of work than he.

As with most Boston furniture of the period, Crehore's surviving pianos, all of the square variety, are patterned after English examples. He emulated the casework of these pianos closely, but was not as slav-

ish with their mechanical workings, introducing a few inventive changes of his own here and there, but none of lasting influence. A recently discovered newspaper advertisement indicates that in 1799 Crehore manufactured at least one example of a grand piano, which is far earlier than was generally believed such instruments were made in America. This graceful Sheraton-style instrument is one of Crehore's best preserved pianos, with lovely floral decoration above the keyboard attributed to John Ritto Penniman, a noted ornamental painter in Boston.

Mahogany case

L. 159.2 cm, w. 56.7 cm, h. 23.7 cm

(L. 62 ¹¹⁄₁₆ in., w. 22 ⅜ in., h. 9 ⁵⁄₁₆ in.)

Gift of Camilla Cunningham Blackman

in Memory of Lucy Clarendon Crehore 1992.95

For Further Reading

Given the tremendous scope of musical instruments as a subject, this list is necessarily limited to very general sources. Many of them contain excellent bibliographies that will lead the reader to more detailed literature about specific instruments and musical genres.

Baines, Anthony. *The Oxford Companion to Musical Instruments*. Oxford: Oxford University Press, 1992.

Bessaraboff, Nicholas. *Ancient European Musical Instruments: An Organological Study of the Musical Instruments in the Leslie Lindsey Mason Collection at the Museum of Fine Arts, Boston*. Cambridge (Mass.): Harvard University Press, 1941.

The Garland Encyclopedia of World Music. New York and London: Garland Publishing, Inc., 1998–2002. Ten volumes.

The New Grove Dictionary of Musical Instruments. London: Macmillan Press Limited, 1984. Three volumes.

Koster, John. *Keyboard Musical Instruments in the Museum of Fine Arts, Boston*. Boston: Museum of Fine Arts, 1994.

Libin, Laurence. *American Musical Instruments in the Metropolitan Museum of Art*. New York and London: W. W. Norton and Company, 1985.

Marcuse, Sibyl. *A Survey of Musical Instruments*. New York: Harper and Row, 1975.

Rault, Lucie. *Musical Instruments: Craftsmanship and Traditions from Prehistory to the Present*. New York: Harry N. Abrahms, Inc., 2000.

Remnant, Mary. *Musical Instruments: An Illustrated History from Antiquity to the Present*. Portland (Ore.), Amadeus Press, 1989.

Index

Page numbers in italics indicate illustrations.